ENGLISCH TRAINING

Josef Kilger

Comprehension 2

Aufgaben mit Lösungen

ab 9. Klasse

STARK

ISBN: 3-89449-144-2

1. Auflage 1994

Inhalt

(Fortsetzung nächste Seite)

Anhang

Autor: Josef Kilger, Konrektor, Konrad-Adenauer-Realschule Roding

Vorwort

Liebe Schülerin, lieber Schüler,

das vorliegende Trainingsmaterial soll dir dabei helfen, Comprehensionaufgaben besser und schneller zu meistern und dich optimal auf **Schulaufgaben** und die **Abschlußprüfung** vorzubereiten. Dieses Ansinnen spiegelt sich auch in seinem Aufbau wider:

- Im **ersten Teil** des Buches findest du am Anfang jeden Kapitels einen **Text,** der deinem Erfahrungsbereich entnommen ist. Schon das Lesen des Textes und der Fragen dazu werden deinen Wortschatz erweitern.

  Es folgen die **Fragen zum Text** sowie **Grammatik-** und **Übersetzungsaufgaben**. Letztere gibt es in großer Zahl, da sie sich sehr gut dazu eignen, deinen Wortschatz zu erweitern.

  Was die Grammatik betrifft, liegt ein Schwerpunkt auf der **indirekten Rede** und der **Zeitenbildung** im **Aktiv** und **Passiv** von Zeitwörtern, denn ohne ihre Kenntnis kannst du keine nichtwörtliche (indirekte) Rede bilden.
- Im **zweiten Teil** des Buches findest du die **Lösungen** zu jedem Kapitel, die du mit denen in deinem Übungsheft vergleichen kannst. Schreibe nicht ins Buch, damit du die eine oder andere Übung wiederholen kannst, solltest du sie beim ersten Mal noch nicht gleich richtig gelöst haben.
- Die **Tabellen** am Ende des Buches helfen dir bei der Zeitenbildung.

Die Verweise im Buch beziehen sich immer auf die Abschnitte B (Worksheet) und C (Solutions).

Frau Erika Griesbeck danke ich herzlich für die Durchsicht des Manuskriptes als native speaker.

Viel Spaß beim Üben!

Josef Kilger

Kapitel 1

A. Text

Is work vital?

Many people and pupils often ask themselves why they have to work, why they must sit in classrooms and are taught by strict teachers, why they can't stay at home. They wonder why they are forced to get up early, why they have the necessary shower in order to wake up, why they have to drink their cups of coffee so hastily. You see you are not free and independent!

While working or listening to the teacher you dream of the South Sea or Caribbean islands. You think of wonderful beaches where you can do what you want to do. You can swim in the sea or simply do nothing. It resembles a paradise.

But your life is quite different. You are sitting in a cage or in a prison. You are chained to school, to maths and chemistry, to the timetable. You depend on your parents who say what you have to do. But don't believe that your dad is totally free. He is also sitting in a cage. The "bars" of the cage which hinder him from escaping are a) the boss, b) the tax office, c) how to finance a new car, d) how to earn more money (and many other problems from e to z).

There is no life without problems (which can be solved). There is no life without work and strain. Work is necessary in order to appreciate your spare time. To be sure, millionaires and billionaires are poor people as their main occupation is how to kill time.

You must work. Take your maths or chemistry book and study it for a fixed period of time every day. After that you can go to the swimming baths. You can either lie in the sun or you can dive and forget the stress. But don't forget the chemical formula for water. By the way, it's H_2O.

B. Worksheet

I. Questions on the text

1. What can't you do as you are chained to your job in the morning?
2. What do you dream of when you are working. Don't simply copy the text.
3. Why isn't your life a paradise?
4. Why isn't your dad in a better position?
5. Why is work necessary?
6. Why might a millionaire's life be more boring than yours?

II. Additional questions

1. Why must you drink your coffee hastily?
2. What do you do when you want to relax?
3. What does an extremely beautiful landscape look like?
4. What kind of books would you like to read if there was plenty of time?
5. What beautiful place would you like to see? Give a "substantial" answer.
6. Why are taxes necessary?
7. In the text you find things and facts grown-ups worry about. Add two more items you might worry about.

III. Translate

1. Ich wünschte, ich wäre in der Südsee!
2. Ich wünschte, ich hätte nicht geträumt!
3 Ich wünschte, mein Chef würde mir einen Tag Urlaub geben!

IV. Infinitive or -ing-form

1. Many people enjoy (wear) ragged jeans.
2. Do you mind (work) overtime?
3. The worker refuses (go) by train.
4. Do you think he manages (earn) enough money?
5. When do you start (work)?
6. Some people think it's a problem (get) up so early.
7. Are you fond of (work) in the office?
8. Mr Gay is very good at (prepare) parties in the firm.

9. Are you used to (hear) the bad marks of your daughter?
10. The workers were very proud of (be) in this firm.
11. Did you dream of (live) in the South Sea?
12. Many people succeeded in (get) much money.
13. Do you object to (work) in the late afternoon?
14. Do you have any opportunity of (go) to England?
15. Mr Flisher entered the firm in the hope of (marry) the boss's daughter. He didn't succeed in (become) the son-in-law of the boss. The daughter was only interested in (marry) a rich man.
16. Translate:
    a) Sobald Mr Flisher die Tochter sah, wollte er sie heiraten.
    b) Mr Clever arbeitete 20 Jahre, ohne Steuern zu bezahlen.
    c) Nachdem das Finanzamt das herausgefunden hatte, mußte er 5651,05 GBP zahlen.

V. Put in the correct tense of the words given in brackets

1. I would be glad if my boss (give) me more money.
2. If I get more salary I (buy) a house in Italy.
3. You must work overtime if more people (want) to buy more articles.
4. I might have plenty of time if I (be) on an island.
5. You could go steady with your girl if she (learn) how to behave.
6. If I had won in the lottery I (not, start) in Mr Strict's firm.
7. If I am invited to the boss's party I (dress) elegantly.
8. I would buy many presents if I (invite) by the boss.
9. I would have watched video films instead of working if I (have) enough money and (give) a big amount of money by my rich uncle.
10. If I have enough money the palace (buy).
11. I would have bought the car if the money (send) to me in time.
12. I would be lucky if I (give) enough money.

VI. Ask the questions

1.
1. Yes, I had to get up early.
2.
2. Yes, he brushes his teeth hastily.
3.
3. Yes, he had bacon and eggs for breakfast.

4.
4. Yes, I was dreaming of the South Sea.
5.
5. Yes, I have paid the bills.
6.
6. No, I needn't pay high taxes.
7.
7. Yes, I was allowed to leave.
8.
8. Yes, I swam in the sea.

VII. Agree

1. I am tired out.
2. I like indoor entertainments.
3. I worked overtime.
4. I arrive and leave as I like.
5. I can't stay at home.
6. I don't like these TV programmes.
7. I didn't earn much money.
8. I haven't worried about that.
9. I won't stop avoiding the rush hour.

Kapitel 2

A. Text

Technical equipment or are computers necessary?

I attended my first class at the elementary school when I saw my first film. Some American soldiers drove their jeeps into the school yard with a trailer. It was the huge machine for producing electrical current using the engine of one of the jeeps. Then they laid out cables, the projector was put on a desk. Everybody was looking forward to watching the first film. Then it began: It was the fable of the hare and the hedgehog. You remember, the hare ran as fast as he could, but when he came to the finishing line, breathless and totally exhausted, the hedgehog was there and waiting for him. Poor hare! He didn't realize the trick of "Mr" and "Mrs" Hedgehog. The film was very short but everybody was enthusiastic. And it was the only film for many years to come. We continued working with textbooks, pencils, the blackboard and chalk. There wasn't even a radio in the classroom let alone a television set. When I started my career as a teacher in the sixties they established huge language labs which cost an immense amount of money. Every pupil sat in a kind of cabin. The pupils were connected with their teacher by means of earphones like puppets on a string. It went like this: Teacher: "The Queen will visit us next Thursday." Pupils: "The Queen will visit us next Thursday." Or the Teacher asked questions and the pupils had to answer. Then the teacher gave the correct answer.

The teacher could hear if everybody spoke correctly by pressing a special button with the number of the cabin. And the pupil could even record this sentence on a tape to hear his voice again. I thought it was a good way of learning a language and even the pupils believed that because it was new technical equipment. Later the enthusiasm for the language labs lessened and the cabins were used for writing test papers. Now these labs, if they still exist at all, are totally out of date and look like dinosaurs of bygone ages. Meanwhile there was a revolution which brought a New Age, the Information Age which supplied us with radios, TV, video recorders and last but not least computers. Will they also be old-fashioned dinosaurs after a time?

Now we have entered this exciting new age, the classroom is changing. The history teacher may put a cassette in the recorder and the pupils can say "oh" or "super" when they see Admiral Nelson saying: "England expects everyman to do his duty." And we can take part when her Majesty the Queen celebrates her official birthday with a big tattoo. I doubt whether pupils have better marks when seeing videos. We use tiny recorders when listening to English texts. The first recorder I owned was very big and extremely heavy with huge reels. You had to be something like a technician in order to use it properly. And we even have the new subject: Informatics or computer science. There are two ways: The more difficult way is to make programmes and handle the computer correctly. Ambition: Computer Operator. The easier way is to learn how to write simple texts and lists. In this case the computer is a "better" typewriter. Professional ambition: Clerk, office worker, secretary. Whether you accept it or not, life without computers is unthinkable. Many private homes have their own computers and in the offices of lawyers, solicitors or notaries, in stores, in surgeries, etc., etc. there are computers, too. So better become friends with them.

B. Worksheet

I. Answer the questions on the text in complete sentences

1. Why did the American soldiers have to use trailers?
2. Why was everybody enthusiastic?
3. What was different in the classrooms of 1990 and 1950?
4. In which way were pupils able to learn English in the sixties?
5. Tell me two advantages of learning English by means of a language lab (oratory)?
6. Why did the pupils accept this new way of learning a language?
7. What was the "trick" of the hedgehogs?
8. Why doesn't the author believe that we will use the present computers for ever? Find the reason in the text.
9. Is the author convinced that you have better history marks when watching videos?
10. Why must you become friends with computers?
11. What are the two substantial parts of computer work?

II. Answer further questions in full sentences as well

1. Why do grown-ups have more problems with computers than you have?
2. Why are parents in favour of teaching informatics at school?
3. Why is it good for you to learn how to use a computer?
4. Can you tell me other fables?
5. Which equipment must you have when you go
   a) skiing
   b) rock climbing
   c) to school?
6. Can the pupils really see Admiral Horatio Nelson?
7. In which way were the cabins "misused" and why didn't the pupils like that?
8. Why did the author use the term **dinosaurs?**

III. Fill in synonyms

1. Many kids have **got used** ... to the new electronic equipment.
2. Even the parents **can't ignore** ... computers.
3. They must admit that a computer is a **remarkably** ... good thing.

4. **At first** ... they were skeptical about it.
5. But nowadays they **enable** ... their children to work with computers.
6. Today computers play an important **role** ... at schools.
7. **In spite of** ... the high expenses they **have to** ... be bought.
8. But many parents **are afraid** ... that their kids will spend all the time with the computer.

IV. Complete the sentences

1. They encouraged (we, use) computers.
2. The teacher wanted (they, buy) that computer.
3. Can the parents count on (she, deal) with the computer programme?
4. Is it important (**preposition**, you, learn) how to write simple texts at least?
5. It's really necessary (**preposition**, everybody, become) friends with computers.
6. It's clever (**preposition**, they, learn) computer work with their kids.

V. Complete once more. Insert the correct preposition:

1. I don't blame (the author, **preposition**, tell) a lot about his youth.
2. Don't object (**preposition**, work) hard every day.
3. How can I prevent the kids (**preposition**, play) computer games?

VI. The correct tense

1. If they hadn't had a machine which produced electricity they (not, see) the film.
2. If the hare (know) that there was a couple of hedgehogs he wouldn't have been tricked.
3. The teacher will hear the pupils' answers if he (press) the button.
4. If teaching by means of the language lab is old-fashioned we (use) the cabins for doing examinations.
5. If the history teacher (be ill) we would watch a video cassette on the Civil War.
6. Shouldn't the teacher come we (occupy) ourselves.

VII. The correct tense

1. Thirty years ago the author (begin) teaching.
2. Since then he (see) many changes.

3. For 15 years the teachers (be) fans of electronic equipment.
4. Next year I (attend) a computer course.
5. After he (buy) a computer he began working immediately.
6. The man (work) at the computer when the door bell rang.

VIII. Ask your friend

1. "Willst Du einen Versuch machen?"
1.
2. "Wird die Schule durch die Computer beeinflußt?"
2.
3. "Müssen wir die neue Technik annehmen?"
3.
4. "Wer versorgt uns mit Software?"
4.

IX. Definitions

1. equipment:
2. jeep:
3. fable:
4. hedgehog:
5. career:
6. dinosaur:
7. revolution:
8. tattoo:
9. lawyer:
10. notary:
11. store:
12. surgery:
13. escape:

X. Find the opposite

1. to lessen
2. old-fashioned
3. finish
4. connect
5. entered
6. official

XI. Complete the list

	Noun	Verb	Adjective
1.		attend	
2.		see	–
3.		–	technical
4.		produce	
5.		–	poor
6.		connect	–
7.	number		
8.		believe	
9.	enthusiasm	–	
10.		exist	
11.			exciting

XII. A minister was talking about computer technology. Some journalists wrote down what he said. Start with:

The minister said (asked) ...

1. "Several years ago only specialists knew how to deal with computers."
2. "Yesterday I visited children in an elementary school who had to use computers."
3. "For many years I've been a fan of computers and the government will finance the equipment at schools."
4. "Everybody must support the new ideal of the Information Age."
5. "You needn't give up reading books as they are as vital as they were before."
6. "Do you believe that computers will be dinosaurs in the next decade?"
7. "When will you publish what I've said?"

Kapitel 3

A. Text

John Earl of Sandwich

Not everything which comes from America may be good. So many people doubt whether the Euro Disneyland in Paris which was opened in 1992 is necessary or vital for Europe and they ask themselves whether it is culture or mere kitsch. This "Empire of Fun" won't be accepted by all Europeans. But other "kingdoms of pleasure" are accepted especially by the kids (and not only by them) who persuade or convince their parents to go there: We deal with the fast-food restaurants which offer minced meat in bread rolls, non-alcoholic drinks, chips and ketchup and use lots of plastic dishes and boxes. Everything is rather quick and many Europeans think we shouldn't eat so quickly. Think of France and Italy where eating is a ceremony. The longer the better!

Two hundred years ago the Minister of the Navy John Montague, Earl of Sandwich died. He was the "Gambling Earl" who spent most of his time at the gambling tables. Sometimes he won a lot, then he lost lots of money. I don't know whether he was addicted to gambling but he played enthusiastically. So he never had time for his lunch or dinner. It was a very exciting game: John Montague, the fourth Earl of Sandwich asked the waiter to bring him a piece of roast beef – some report it was veal – between two slices of bread. So the Earl could hold the food in one hand and continue playing for 24 hours. So the **sandwich** got its name and since then we have consumed this sort of food. Later they introduced many variations: Different sorts of meat were used, e. g. ham, or you can spread butter or use cheese. You may add one or two lettuce leaves or slices of tomato or cucumber. The most famous sandwich is the French **baguette**, a long narrow loaf "filled" with ham and cheese and other different delicious things. You can even have lobster or salmon or sardine sandwiches, etc., etc. And don't forget ingredients such as mustard, saffron, ginger or coriander. We don't know who the champion is, the **hamburger** of the fast-food restaurant or the baguette, but John Montague, the fourth Earl of Sandwich, created this sort of food as he wanted one hand to be free for gambling.

B. Worksheet

I. Questions on the text

1. Why can't many Europeans stand amusement centres like the Euro Disney?
2. Why are some people against fast-food-restaurants?
3. Why must many children persuade or convince their parents to go there?
4. What should be abolished in these restaurants?
5. What was John Montague, Earl of Sandwich, in charge of?
6. Why was he called the Gambling Earl?
7. Can you see from the text whether he was an addict or only an enthusiast?
8. Tell me in your own words in which way the sandwich came into existence.
9. "John Earl of Sandwich lost many games but he never lost his appetite." Is it a true or a false statement?
10. What's the difference between the original sandwich and a French baguette?
11. Say in your own words what **champion** means here?
12. What does your younger sister say when she finds the fast-food restaurant really good?
13. Why did the Earl have a waiter of his own? Where else do you find waiters and waitresses?

II. Additional questions

1. Do you think the Euro Disneyland is culture or kitsch? Or is it necessary or not? What are the advantages or disadvantages of such an entertainment centre?
2. What else can you "fill" a sandwich with?
3. Why are kids fans of fast-food restaurants? And not only kids!
4. Why are many persons against fast-food like this?
5. There are things which speak up for fast-food restaurants. Tell me.
6. What's the difference between a fast-food restaurant and a snack-bar or kiosk?
7. Explain the "ceremony" of Italian or French dining.
8. Define what **addicted to gambling** means: What else can you be addicted to? Can we help those people and how?
9. What are the differences between **sandwich**, baguette or hamburger?

10. What do you think a snob sandwich is?
11. What sort of people may sometimes prefer this sort of fast food despite their preferring dining out occasionally?
12. What's the difference between the menu on your computer screen (monitor) and the menu in a restaurant?
13. What's the difference between a recipe and a prescription?
14. Find two reasons why people are vegetarians.
15. What sacrifices must people make who want to get slim?

III. Definitions

1. Culture:
2. Empire of fun:
3. chips:
4. minister:
5. gambling:
6. earl:
7. beef:
8. lobster:
9. ingredients:

IV. Agree

1. "A hamburger is great." ...
2. "I don't like baguettes." ...
3. "I was in the Euro Disneyland." ...
4. "She wore a Mickey Mouse badget." ...

V. Mixed Grammar Passage: Now we are leaving fast-food-restaurants and are talking about Paul Bocuse, the famous chef

1. If P. B. opened a restaurant in my town I ...(be) his enthusiastic customer.
2. Many of my friends ... (become) chefs if they had had the opportunity ... (get) an apprenticeship.
3. I would ... (real) enjoy ... (be) a chef and I wouldn't hesitate ... (help) P. B. in the kitchen.
4. Since 1985 I ... (study) cookbooks and I have ... (usual) prepared many dinners myself.
5. Last Sunday I ... (find) an interesting recipe and made a dinner which tasted ... (delicious).

6. I invited P. B. but up to now my invitation letter ... (not, answer).
7. Of course there are several ways ... (garnish) a dish.
8. You can take lettuce ... (leaf) or a bayleaf.
9. There is no difficulty ...(do) that.
10. P. B. said that in his restaurant the pears and strawberries ... (taste) ... (extraordinary, excellent) and every customer was ... (whole) satisfied.
11. Some younger customers say there are the ... (charming) waitresses of the world who serve the meals ... (friendly).
12. But others say there are the ... (elegant) girls.

Once more I want to tell you something about my dinners.

13. Before ... (lay) the table I decorated it with flowers.
14. I can do that ... (mechanic) as I do it very often.
15. And I laid the table ... (extreme, careful).
16. For many years not one glass ... (break)!

VI. Now we aren't filling our sandwiches, we have to fill in the same or similar expressions in the gaps

1. Some people can't **stand** ... fast-food restaurants.
2. Some parents believe they can **relax** ... in a fast-food restaurant.
3. **As a matter of fact**, ... lots of boys and girls like hamburgers.
4. Who is **keen on** ... baguettes?
5. Many **ask themselves** ... if amusement centres are necessary.
6. A hamburger is a **sort** ... of food.
7. You needn't **lose your temper** ... when I say I'm a hamburger fan.
8. A baguette is not a **simple** ... sandwich.
9. Some kids believe they are **up to date** ... when they **prefer** ... baguettes.
10. Only **a few** ... parents are **courageous** ... enough not to go there.
11. But others are **mean** ...
12. You must eat your sandwich rather **fast** ...
13. But many **believe** ... you **shouldn't** ... do so.
14. Sometimes the Earl won **a lot of** ... money.
15. It was **a characteristic** ... of the Earl to spend most of his time at the gambling tables.
16. **Sometimes** ... he lost money.
17. He was eating and able to **continue** ... with the games.
18. The **most famous** ... sandwich is the baguette.
19. Sandwich **created** ... this food more than two hundred years ago.

Kapitel 4

A. Text

The earthquake or where have you been?

My name is David Fair. Last year I bought a new car as I had saved money for five years and didn't spend it on going out or buying elegant suits. It was red and I drove proudly through my native town. But there was my brother John. He was an apprentice with an insurance company and got acquainted with the most beautiful girl so far I can tell. Monica was slim, had long fair hair, wore black leggings and mini skirts. John had a new girl but no car. I had a car but no girl as she had left me some weeks before. The reader may understand that I lent my car to Lucky John as he wanted to go dancing in the neighbouring town.

I was sitting in the living-room listening to the radio. It said that there was a serious earthquake which woke people up who then got into a panic and ran out of their houses. Many were injured slightly, some seriously. Chimneys fell down onto the streets, bricks hit people and cars. Many people had to be taken to hospital. Some extremely nervous people and those suffering from heart diseases were given stabilizing pills or injections. The police and the fire brigade were phoned continually and asked for help and advice on what to do. The Atomic Power Plant was switched off immediately when they noticed that the earth was shaking.

After ten minutes the telephone rang. "John speaking." His voice sounded extraordinarily sad. "There are some red bricks on the car and lots of sand", he told me. And on the driver's seat there are two tiles.

Next morning I went to the neighbouring town by bus and had my damaged car towed off by a breakdown van. They took it to the garage. Fortunately there was an insurance against earthquakes and so the car could be repaired without any cost to me. My brother John, the clever apprentice, had persuaded me to take out an insurance against earthquakes. His boss thanked him because of this first contract and I myself must thank him, too. I think he is a good apprentice and will be a good insurance broker some day.

Last Sunday I went out with Monica. She probably thinks I am more interesting and dance much better than John. There isn't any insurance against girls leaving their friends, poor John. What happened to John won't happen to me!

B. Worksheet

I. Questions on the text

1. Why could D. F. afford to buy a new car?
2. Which trade did his brother learn?
3. Did Monica's way of dressing improve her outward appearance?
4. Why did John ask his brother for his car? There is more than one reason:
5. Describe what damage an extremely bad earthquake may cause. Think of the 1907 earthquake in San Francisco or other catastrophes.
6. Which group of people is extremely endangered in an earthquake?
7. Why must an atomic power plant be switched off?
8. Why was John in a bad mood when he phoned his brother and why was David's mood not better after that?
9. Why did D. F. think his younger brother was a skilful apprentice to an insurance broker?
10. Why did John's boss thank Fair's brother and why did Fair have to thank him?
11. Do you believe that D. F. can go steady with Monica?
12. What didn't D. F. see as he didn't watch TV that day?
13. Why were the police phoned continuously?
14. Which parts of the car must have been broken as there were tiles on the driver's seat?
15. Which parts of the car had to be repaired or replaced in the garage?

II. Additional questions

1. What can you insure yourself against apart from earthquakes?
2. Draw a picture of your favourite boy or girl: What must he (she) look like? Which qualities must he (she) have?
3. Why may a girl or boy end a romance?
4. Why do young people go to discos?
5. When else must you be helped by a breakdown van?
6. Try to convince me that I need this or that insurance? Take any as example.
7. What can you do to attract the attention of a girl or boy?
8. What can you say to a girl or boy when you want to get acquainted with her (him)?
9. What can you advise me if my girl or friend has left me?

10. What must you make sure of when you allow a friend to use your car?
11. Why are insurances or assurances vital or necessary?
12. Why do you think there is love at first sight?
13. Why can't we do away with cars in spite of traffic jams and pollution?

III. Definitions

1. native town:
2. apprentice:
3. insurance company:
4. mini skirt:
5. earthquake:
6. panic:
7. hospital:
8. injection:
9. insurance contract

IV. Infinitive or -ing-form

1. You can't avoid ... (be) the victim of an earthquake.
2. Did you manage ... (invite) the girl to the dancing party?
3. He didn't mind ... (give) his car to his brother.
4. He often attempted ... (win) the girl back.
5. The company refused ... (pay) the sum.
6. The girl enjoyed ... (dance) with him.
7. Keep ... (be) friendly.
8. The girl wanted ... (dance) with me.
9. Do you like ... (go) by car?
10. He continued ... (be) self-confident.

V. Decide whether you take oneself or one another: There is no emphatic use

1. He hurt ... when he wanted to help his neighbour.
2. After the earthquake the police and the mayor met ... yesterday.
3. "Why can't you behave ...", the girl complained at the dancing party.
4. They talked ... for a very long time.
5. Do you remember ... Monica.
6. Many people complained ... about the authorities.
7. Monica and John don't like ... any more.

8. The people comforted ... after the earthquake.
9. It's no use hiding ... in the basement during an earthquake.

VI. Übersetzungspassage

Zur Einübung der Grammatik (Frage, Verneinung, rückbezügliches Fürwort) ist auch eine Übersetzung sinnvoll. Beachte, daß nicht in allen Fällen das rückbezügliche Fürwort (Reflexive Pronoun) genommen werden darf:

1. Amüsierten sich die jungen Leute in der Disco?
2. Ich stellte mich Monica nicht vor.
3. Paßte sie sich ihm an?
4. Mußtest du dich ändern?
5. Erinnerst du dich an den ersten Kuß?
6. Wir interessierten uns nicht für die anderen.
7. Freust du dich nicht über die Verabredung?
8. Seit zwei Jahren kümmert er sich um sie.
9. Nimmt sie es auf sich, seine schlechten Eigenschaften zu ertragen?
10. Wann müssen wir uns verabschieden?

VII. Eine weitere Übersetzungspassage

soll den Unterschied zwischen dem rückbezüglichen und dem betonendem Fürwort oder dem Reflexive und dem Emphasizing Pronoun herausstellen. Du kannst vorweg auch den Lösungsvorspann durchlesen.

1. Du kannst das Auto nicht selber reparieren.
2. Er fuhr den Wagen selber in die Werkstatt.
3. Der Chef interessierte sich selber für den Schaden.
4. Irrte er sich?
5. Der Fahrer ärgerte sich.
6. "Ich kann mich selber entschuldigen", sagte er.
7. Das Auto näherte sich von selber, da die Handbremse nicht funktionierte.
8. Der Fahrer entschuldigte sich.
9. Er ärgerte sich selber.
10. Die Geschichte ereignete sich gestern.

VIII. Translation passage

Decide whether you can take **one another** or **each other**. If you don't know what to do read the "leader" of the solutions first.

1. Monica und ich konnten uns lange Zeit nicht sehen.
2. Aber dann trafen wir uns jeden Tag.
3. Wir küßten uns herzlich und schauten uns liebevoll an.
4. Wir stritten niemals.
5. Wir fragten uns, warum sich andere Paare trennten.
6. "Kommt ihr gut miteinander aus"? fragten unsere Freunde.
7. Bald verlobten wir uns und heirateten.
8. Bei der Hochzeit stellten sich die Verwandten einander vor.
9. Wir wollen immer miteinander reden, sogar wenn es schwerfällt.
10. Wenn sie sich immer (gegenseitig) helfen, werden sie sich nicht scheiden lassen.

Kapitel 5

A. Text

The man was furious indeed

After a hard day's work and the strenuous visit of his brother-in-law he simply wanted to sleep. He went to bed immediately after he had said good-bye to his nerve-racking visitor. Usually he read some pages of his favourite book "The Rise and Fall of the Roman Empire", but this day he didn't do what he used to do. He switched off his bedside-lamp and fell asleep. The reader may ask me whether he was a bachelor as I didn't mention his wife. He was married, in fact. But that day his wife was away from home. She was seeing her former classmates. They came together every four weeks.

After about one hour he was woken up by a strange noise. It sounded like breaking glass. His first thought was that somebody wanted to enter his house through a window – not through the front door where there was a bell for visitors! The noise came from the back garden. He took a torch and his toy pistol and went outside. He watched and listened but he didn't see or hear anybody. There wasn't a window damaged, so he returned and went to bed after locking every door twice.

At midnight his wife came home from the restaurant. After she had given her husband a hearty kiss she told him that the council workers had put up two big containers that afternoon opposite their back garden. The council is the owner of that site. His wife told him that one container was for bottles and glasses and jars, the other one for newspapers and magazines.

Although there was a big yellow sticker saying DON'T THROW IN BOTTLES AFTER 8 PM somebody had thrown his bottles into the container and caused a lot of trouble.

I think everybody must be in favour of protecting the environment but the people living next to the containers aren't very pleased about them. Actually, reckless people throw in glasses when they like and when our man came home from work on one of the following days both containers were full and on the ground there were lots of bottles in boxes and cases and piles of newspapers and magazines. It was really a mess.

During the night it rained extremely heavily and a storm arose so the newspapers were scattered on this man's garden. Even in the trees and bushes there were scraps of paper.

What can you learn from that?

B. Worksheet

I. Answer the questions on the text in complete sentences

1. Answer in your own words why our man wanted to go to bed?
2. Was he married and if so where was his wife?
3. What did he think first after hearing the noise of breaking glass?
4. When was he informed about where the noise came from?
5. Why was the council allowed to put containers there?
6. Who causes a lot of trouble?
7. There wasn't only noise, there was also a terrible mess. Can you tell me why?

II. Answer the additional questions in full sentences as well

1. What do you think a nerve-racking visitor is?
2. What is a favourite book?
3. Why must you lock a door?
4. Why was there a sticker on the glass container?
5. What can you do when you are in favour of protecting the environment?
6. What can you really learn from that?

III. Put in the correct tense of the word in brackets

1. Yesterday my sister-in-law ... (visit) me.
2. She ... (live)Kent now.
3 Since 1990 my wife ... (met) her classmates.
4. My father-in-law ... (be) mayor of the town from 1960 to 1972 after he ... (be) a member of the council.
5. For many years I ... (be) a member of the council (up to now).
6. By next year we ... (build) the new recycling yard and ... (construct) two garbage dumps.
7. Next month we ... (replace) the containers by bigger ones.
8. After he ... (realise) that the container was full the reckless neighbour usually (put) the empty bottles outside it.
9. While he ... (do) so yesterday I adressed him.
10. He ... (lose) his temper at once, as he usually ... (lose) it. It's a pity.

IV. Write down what the mayor said the day before

The mayor said:

1. "We are keen on composting waste."
2. "There is a law which forbids throwing litter away."
3. "Tomorrow there will be a lecture on the disadvantages of artificial fertilizers."
4. "We must use farm animal waste."
5. "We mustn't use pesticides."
6. "We can make the soil fertile."
7. "Protection of (the) environment is absolutely necessary."
8. "This has been the best way up to now."
9. "In spite of this I don't like these freaks who only eat muesli."
10. "Last year I visited an area for alternative technology."
11. "By the year 2010 we will have built many solar panels."
12. "We may use our resources but we must use them carefully."
13. "They should do organic gardening only."
14. "After they had realised the advantages they changed their minds."
15. "Now I am going to welcome my friends from our twin town."

Kapitel 6

A. Text

Sport

When his parents moved to the neighbouring town Maximilian had to leave his school. The new school was a huge grey building but it was surrounded by a park. His new fellow pupils welcomed him in a friendly way and so far I can tell he was completely accepted.

The first lesson on the timetable was P. E. The other boys of his class were allowed to sit down on the floor of the gymnasium and Max had to do gym quite alone. The teacher was sitting on the long horse and telling Max what to do. He had to rotate his arms, bend his knees, bend his body, do a hand-stand, do cart-wheels, etc. The result was that Max didn't like sport in the gym. The day when P. E. was on the time-table was simply "spoilt". Only in summer he didn't dislike sport, he even liked the short- and long-distance races in the open air.

When Max was fifty years old he did gymnastics with a class. You may understand that he wasn't a P. E. teacher, but the P. E. teacher was in hospital and Max replaced her during this period. Before they started a game of volleyball Max and the pupils ran around the gym, Max in front and the pupils behind him. But suddenly Max felt a pain in his right leg as if somebody had hit him. He looked back but the pupils were ten metres behind him. Then he sat down on a bench as he couldn't walk any longer.

Dr. Miller examined him carefully and made the decision that he had to be operated on: The Achilles tendon was damaged! (You know the story of Achilles of the Trojan War.) This tendon is like a string or a spring which extends and compresses when a runner runs and therefore produces energy. Modern running shoes have got air pockets which make this energy greater. The crux of the matter was that Max wasn't wearing running shoes (or simply shoes) when he was running. He was barefoot!

After the operation he had to stay in hospital for many weeks. His right foot was bandaged and put in plaster. The girls of the class often came to see him and brought flowers and trinkets. They just stood in the room and didn't say a lot. They simply expected the teacher to speak.

Don't forget: Unlucky accidents shouldn't discourage you in sport. P. E. is the first step for the Olympic Games.

B. Worksheet

I. Questions on the text

1. Why were the surroundings of the new school friendlier or more attractive?
2. Say in your own words: *he was completely accepted.*
3. Do you think that the P. E. teacher was a kind teacher?
4. Have you got any idea why the teacher treated Max in such a bad way?
5. What was the inevitable consequence of this treatment?
6. Was there an inner connection between Max's treatment and his dislike of P. E.?
7. Could you imagine there was a very good atmosphere in the P. E. teachers's class?
8. Why did Max take a P. E. lesson, when he was 50?
9. Why did the girls and Max run before the match?
10. Why couldn't any of the pupils hit their teacher?
11. Why was Max in a greater danger of damaging his Achilles tendon?
12. Why weren't the girls accustomed to telling their teacher a lot?

II. Additional questions

1. Why must people move? Find two reasons.
2. What do you actually do when you leave
   a) school,
   b) a firm,
   c) friends?
3. What is a park. What can you do in a park?
4. What do the letters P. E. stand for?
5. Why didn't Max want to be a P. E. teacher?
6. Why is a person in hospital?
7. Who enabled Max to walk again?
8. How long was Max handicapped?
9. What could have happened if the surgeon hadn't been capable?
10. You want to visit somebody in the hospital, what can you take with you?
11. Would you like to have more P. E. lessons or more German lessons?. Why do you think are there opponents to the increase of P. E. lessons?
12. What do you think about the many accidents in P. E. lessons? Are they inevitable?

13. Is it true that **sport is a science**? (Think of the Olympic Games, the hard sports, stream-lining, tight swimsuits, doping, special food).

III. Further questions

1. Why do so many national teams compete against each other in the Olympics?
2. Where does the Olympic flame come from?

IV. Write down what the reporter said. Start with:

The reporter said (that)...

1. A burning arrow lit the Olympic flame.
2. The XXV Summer Olympics were opened by the Spanish monarch Juan Carlos.
3. More than 170 national teams will take part.
4. Some nations returned as they were absent.
5. Some teams think they can use the games to get a better reputation.
6. They have replaced older members of the teams by younger ones.
7. The organizers emphasize that any dope must be forbidden.
8. This sort of stimulus mustn't be accepted.
9. This year everybody, the competitors and the coach look confident.
10. Now I am talking to sprinter A. B. who arrived here yesterday.
11. M. B. has been the fastest swimmer up to now.
12. Next year I will write a book on the athletes.

V. Say in a different way using the -ing-form

1. **As soon as he heard** about the modern running shoes he bought them.
2. **While she was sitting** in the cafeteria she was listening to the radio reports.
3. **After he had won** the long-distance run he kissed the ground.
4. **Before she does** her vaulting exercises she always has a light meal.
5. **Since the runner wears** a T-shirt with the slogan SAY NO TO DRUGS he is heartily applauded.
6. **If she is invited** to the opening ceremony she is extremely lucky.
7. **When she arrived** at the airport she waved her hands enthusiastically.
8. **After he had run** the marathon he merely wanted to have a cup of tea.
9. **As Mr Biondi is a** fast swimmer he is always surrounded by his fans.
10. **As she doesn't like** publicity she often stays in her hotel.

VI. Translate

1. Abgesehen davon, daß sie einige kleine Fehler machte, kann sie auf eine Medaille hoffen.
2. Sie fürchtet Fehltritte, trotzdem ist sie optimistisch.
3. Anstatt in den Cafeterias herumzusitzen, beobachtet unser Korrespondent alle Disziplinen.
4. Sie sprach davon, ohne zu erröten.
5. Sie hofft zu gewinnen, indem (dadurch, daß) sie einen enganliegenden Badeanzug trägt.
6. Indem (dafür, daß) er viele Athleten untersuchte, erhielt er die Bezeichnung Dopinginspektor.

VII. Mixed Grammar Passage

1. She was running ... (extraordinary, fast).
2. Of course she is used ... (run) after she ... (to be fond) of it for many years.
3. I know it sounds ... (silly) but it's ... (complete) true she can never go ... (slow).
4. She ... (be) in a hurry since she began ... (walk).
5. By the way she is ... (particular) beautiful, she looks ... (good) and her fans are keen on ... (see) her.
6. She doesn't get letters ... (occasional) she gets them ... (frequent).
7. ... (natural) she must train ... (hard).
8. We can rely on her ... (win) gold.
9. Everybody looks forward to ... (take) part in the Olympics and we insist on ... (get) tickets.
10. We think she will run ... (quick) than the world champion.
11. She will do the vaulting ... (good) than the African competitors.
12. She will do them ... (extreme, good).
13. We'll watch the event (special, enthusiastic).

Kapitel 7

A. Text

Stay at home

Everybody knows that the environment is seriously threatened by the exhaust gases of factories and cars. A lot of plans have been made to reduce the stress on nature. Gases have to pass through filters, cars must have special devices to make the burden on nature smaller. If your car hasn't got a catalytic converter you will be burdened with heavier taxes. You can even hear about politicians who suggest taxing oil and petrol even more heavily than it is taxed at the moment. Stop. They have increased the taxes during the last years, in fact.

But dont't forget the tourists. I don't mean their airplanes, cars and buses (see above) which spoil our nature, which stand in endless queues in traffic jams on the motorway. I am thinking of the tourists themselves! I don't want to talk about the exhaust fumes of their cars, I simply want to tell you something about the holidaymakers. Travels have become cheaper and we earn a lot more. In places where you found only a small group of enthusiasts you see crowds of people now. When the tourists have left the place of interest the wardens have to gather a lot of waste: tins, cigarette packets and filter tips, banana skins, bottles, plastic containers.

You can even find fast-food stalls near castles and cathedrals, and many historic buildings are surrounded by souvenir shops. In many Italian towns there are traders offering belts and purses and leather handbags in front of the **palazzi** and cathedrals. The local people are angry about the tourists, who occupy the seats in the restaurants, who overcrowd the streets and squares. (An old proverb says: "When in Rome do as Romans do." The tourists don't do as the Romans do. They only wear bikinis when they enter churches, gentlemen in sportswear sit in elegant restaurants, some don't even wear shirts.)

The text in brackets clearly shows that we can also deal with the protection of culture and civilisation, not only with the environment.

Of course, tourism causes some damage. But we must find a compromise between the wishes of the tourists and the environment as well as between host and guest. We can't always do what we want to do. A famous rococo church in Upper Bavaria is being seriously damaged by the respiration and transpiration of the crowds of visitors. There are plans to close down the building for some period of the day. (Maybe you have heard about the Egyptian government which finally closed King Tut's tomb.)

B. Worksheet

I. Answer the questions on the text in complete sentences

1. What is damaging the environment?
2. What about the tax when you have got a catalytic converter?
3. Why can more people go on holiday?
4. Answer generally what the tourists leave behind?
5. Name two things which arose as a consequence of tourism especially in Italy?
6. Why don't many natives like the visitors?
7. Say in your own words what the compromise could look like?
8. Say in your own words why buildings were closed or will be closed?

II. Answer the additional questions in full sentences as well

1. What can you do to reduce the strain on (the) environment?
2. Why do you think there are plans to tax petrol or to raise the price of it?
3. When are there the longest traffic jams?
4. In the text there is a list of things tourists throw away. What else could the wardens gather?
5. Say in your own words what the proverb "When in Rome ..." means.
6. What do you think about the behaviour of some tourists?
7. What can we do so that tourism is no longer a threat to the environment?

III. Make a list of both simple form and progressive form (continuous form), active

1. present
2. past
3. present perfect
4. past perfect
5. future
6. future perfect
7. conditional
8. conditional perfect

She travels etc.

IV. Translation passage

Read the notes in the solution passage Kap. 7, III first. You don't translate the words in the brackets. They help you to find the correct translation.

1. Der Tourist entspannte sich (Tatsache).
2. Sie wird die Schönheit der Insel bemerken (Tatsache).
3 Seit Jahren steigt der Benzinpreis (wirklich).
4. Er protestiert (gerade) gegen die Unterbringung.
5. Seit 1980 verbringt er den Urlaub in der Toscana (Tatsache).
6. Ich werde meine Urlaubsbekanntschaft anrufen (extra!).
7. Bis 1999 werde ich alle Länder Europas besucht haben (erwartete Tatsache).
8. Sie würden die Touristen übersehen (Tatsache).
9. Sie sammeln den Abfall ein (tatsächliche Aufgabe).
10. Der Tourist küßte seine Freundin (lange).
11. Als er in der Bar einen Campari trank, läutete auf einmal das Telefon (Unterbrechung).
12. (Bis) morgen werden ich mich (seit) drei Wochen hier aufgehalten haben (wirklich).
13. Sie hatten diese Fluglinie genommen (Tatsache).
14. Sie waren durch die Straßen gegangen (lange, in der Hitze).
15. Sie hätten mit dem Einheimischen gesprochen, falls er ... (Tatsache).

V. Make a list of both simple form and progressive form, passive. See exercises above

They are welcomed etc.

VI. Translation

(nur die einfache Form verwenden!)

1. Die Umwelt wurde belastet.
2. Die Steuer wird erhöht.
3. Seit 5 Jahren werden Lederhandtaschen verkauft.
4. Der Abfall war eingesammelt worden.
5. Die Zahl der Touristen wird begrenzt werden.
6. Die Verschmutzung würde verhindert werden.
7. Alles wäre harmonisiert worden.
8. Die Umwelt wird nicht bedroht werden.
9. Bis 2010 wird das Gebäude nicht restauriert (worden) sein!

Kapitel 8

A. Text

The Club

Everybody knows that the emancipation of women is a typical characteristic of the twentieth century. The idea that the sexes are equal began early in this century and has prospered since then. There are many reasons for this development and even the strictest chauvinist or macho must accept the fact that there are women in almost every trade and profession, they have equal voting rights with male voters, there are female Members of Parliament, and there was even a lady Prime Minister in Great Britain.

But Margaret Thatcher, the "Iron Lady" might not have been allowed to enter one of London's male empires, the clubs. I think that even Her Majesty the Queen isn't permitted to enter. (Some have opened their doors to ladies as they didn't have enough members and therefore financial problems). But these tolerated ladies don't have the same rights as the male members. They are excluded from the bar or the smoking-room and don't have the same voting rights. They can vote for the members of the Parliament (which is itself the most exclusive club in the world!) but they can't vote in general meetings of the club.

One of the fortresses or bastions of the male sex might be the Garrick. The members of this club are still defending their outpost against the attacks of the female sex. The Garrick is a symbol of tradition. A tremendous majority rejected the "reform bill" admitting ladies as members.

A club might be a refuge or "shelter" that keeps out any danger or harm. The members are among themselves and aren't disturbed by their girlfriends and wives. There isn't any envy and jealousy. They are like "big boys" who can do what they want or they can simply do nothing. There is no daughter or son who can't do his homework or has got problems, there isn't any argument about the TV programme or anything else. Even happily-married husbands with well-educated children sometimes want to stay out during the night (or only in the evening). It's like being on holiday!

Do you think I am right that such "holidaymakers" aren't fanatic male chauvinists who think that men are better than women? Or is the Garrick one of the clubs which is a bastion against the united forces of female emancipation and female sex?

B. Worksheet

I. Answer the questions on the text in complete sentences

1. What is a typical feature of our century?
2. Give three items which show that there has been any equality of the sexes?
3. Where are ladies usually not allowed to enter?
4. Why did some clubs permit ladies to enter?
5. Why ist the Garrick a symbol of tradition?
6. Say in your own words why a club is a "shelter" or an island which keeps away (the) problems?
7. Read the last paragraph and decide whether I am right.

II. Answer the additional questions in full sentences as well

1. The sexes are equal. Say in your own words what that means.
2. Whom would you call an "Iron Person"?
3. How can you become a Member of Parliament?
4. What's the difference between a club like the Garrick and a tennis club?
5. When else is a shelter vital?
6. Name three more problems a husband has to deal with?
7. What are the clubs and the ladies compared with in the text?

III. Change into the passive

1. The strictest macho accepts it.
2. He will accept it.
3. The president of the club didn't allow that.
4. Some have opened the doors.
5. Some haven't opened them.
6. We had tolerated it.
7. The gentlemen are drinking a martini in the bar.
8. They were defending their male bastion.
9. We must reject this bill.
10. They can reject it.
11. The shelter might (could) keep out problems.
12. The members of the club gave the ladies flowers.
13. The president has given them the member cards.

14. They sent the cards to the absent members.
15. The amused gentlemen looked at the new female members.
16. Even the most stubborn macho didn't laugh at them.
17. Do the wives disturb their husbands?
18. Did they educate their children well?
19. Have they accepted it?

IV. Complete the list

	Verb	Noun	Adjective
1.	to know		–
2.		emancipation	–
3.			characteristic
4.	–		equal
5.	to prosper		
6.		development	–
7.	–		strict
8.		iron	
9.	to enter		–
10.	to think		
11.	to tolerate		–
12.	to defend		–
13.	–	tradition	
14.	to refuse		–
15.		envy	
16.		argument	–
17.	to marry		–
18.	–		fanatic
19.	–		true

V. Definitions

1. emancipation:
2. century:
3. chauvinist (macho):
4. profession:
5. Prime minister:
6. empire:
7. majority:

8. jealousy
9. a happily-married husband

VI. Ask for the given answers

1. a)
   b) Yes, there are many clubs.
2. a)
   b) Yes, they were accepted.
3. a)
   b) Yes, he likes his club.
4. a)
   b) Yes, he was against ladies.
5. a)
   b) Yes, he opposed.
6. a)
   b) Yes, the plan has been rejected.
7. a)
   b) No, they needn't pay a fee.
8. a)
   b) Yes, the plan had to be turned down.
9. a)
   b) Yes, the ladies have to leave.
10. a)
    b) Yes, they will come back.

Kapitel 9

A. Text

Henry VIII

Oh Henry! Even if you aren't good at English you might have heard of Henry VIII, King of England, who had six wives and is the founder of the (High) Church of England or the Anglican faith.

In a portrait at the age of 50 years he is a very unfriendly and extremely fat person. But everybody was younger some time. When he was young he was a charming young prince who was tall, capable and gifted. His first wife was the Spanish Princess Catherine of Aragon (practically his sister-in-law, as she had been married to Henry's brother Arthur, who had died). After sixteen years of marriage to his wife only a daughter was born (Mary). But the king wanted to have a son as an heir to the kingdom. A monarch had to have a male successor who could take over the crown. If there wasn't any, civil wars might arise!

Henry got to know Anne Boleyn. Oh Anne, if you hadn't met Henry your young life wouldn't have ended so abruptly! Anne was young, had wonderful black hair and Henry intended to divorce Catherine and to marry the young Anne. The Pope in Rome couldn't dissolve the marriage but Henry finally got his divorce and declared himself the head of the Church (of England). It was a simple trick in order to change things in fact. Anne was with a child when Great Harry married her. But she also gave birth to a daughter (Elizabeth). In the great film "A man for all seasons", the story about Thomas More, the Chancellor of the Kingdom, you are shocked by the disappointing scene, when the Queen's ladies shout: "It's a girl."

The beautiful Anne wasn't lucky any more. I think she wasn't even happy. Great Harry (it was his pet name) believed the rumours that she was unfaithful, that she had been given roses. The Tower of London witnessed her execution. It was a sunny day (at least in the film) when her life ended. One of the best and experienced French executioners was invited to chop Anne's head off with a sword. The witnesses agreed that he did his job extremely well indeed. Great Henry didn't want the Queen to be executed with an ordinary axe in the ordinary way. What concession and friendliness!

Catherine of Aragon had died before her "successor" ended her young life on Tower Green. So Henry was "free" in each respect. He invited Jane Seymour, they became engaged and married immediately afterwards, still in May. She gave him the prince he had wanted for many years (Edward). But the mother herself died as she had caught a cold.

In order to complete my list of Great Harry's six wives: Number four was Anne of Cleves, a German Princess, Catherine Howard was his fifth wife (she was executed, too) and Catherine Parr became Nr. 6 who finally outlived him. O Harry!

B. Worksheet

I. Answer the questions on the text in complete sentences

1. What did Henry VIII found?
2. Is there any difference between his age of 50 and about 20?
3. Why could he marry his sister-in-law?
4. Why was a prince (not a princess) vital for the kingdom?
5. Why did the king fall in love with Anne?
6. Why were the new Queen's ladies disappointed?
7. Why was Anne sentenced to death and executed?
8. Why was the French executioner invited to do the bloody job?
9. Why was Henry "free" in each respect?
10. Henry VIII. gained what he wanted but at the same time he had to mourn a loss. Tell me.
11. Who died later, Henry or Catherine Parr?
12. Haven't I slipped up when naming the king "Harry"?

II. Answer further questions in full sentences as well

1. Why do you think have you heard about Henry VIII?
2. What must a married man or woman do first when he or she wants to marry again?
3. Can you tell me other civil wars in history or of our time?
4. What's a "successor" in a love story?
5. Why was it a good trick of Henry to declare himself head of the new Church of England?
6. What does an unfaithful partner do?
7. When can you catch a cold?
8. How many of the king's wives were executed?

III. Translation passage

1. Der König ließ sich malen.
2. Er ließ die Königin hinrichten.
3. Er ließ die Prinzessin im Zimmer warten.
4. Er ließ Anna von Kleve im Zimmer zurück.
5. Meine Eltern lassen mich ins Kino gehen, um den Film "Ein Mann für alle Jahreszeiten" anzusehen.
6. Läßt du dir die Haare schneiden, bevor du ins Kino gehst?
7. Nein, ich lasse sie mir nicht schneiden. Ich will lange Haare wie Anne Boleyn haben.

IV. Indirect questions

1. The king asked, "Where is the portrait painter who must paint my portrait"?
2. "When did you hear about these rumours?"
3. "Who was sent to France to invite this executioner?"
4. "Did you receive flowers yesterday, Anne?"
5. "Can we go hunting in the New Forest?"
6. "May I invite you?"
7. "Is this the German princess?"
8. "Have you seen my collection of paintings?"
9. "Will you marry me next year?"
10. "Should we play the lute?"
11. "Shall I sing the song here?"

V. Tell me what the king ordered

1. The king ordered her, "Come to the palace."
2. He commanded them, "Don't show any mercy."
3. He said, "Stay in your chamber."
4. He commanded (us), "Don't talk about what you have heard."

VI. Mixed Grammar Passage

1. Is this princess worth ... (love)?
2. What about ... (go) hunting?
3. I think it's no use ... (wait).
4. "I used to ... (stay) there in winter."
5. If Catherine ... (give) birth to a prince the king wouldn't have asked the pope.
6. The monarch didn't allow ... (she) to get flowers.
7. "I wish the Italian princess ... (is) here but she is in Milan."
8. He was ... (extreme) furious.
9. He didn't mind ... (write) a lot of love letters a day.
10. "This information tastes ... (bitter)".
11. "You can't avoid ... (be executed).
12. She expected ... (be released).
13. Nobody managed ... (rescue) the queen.
14. The crowd was ... (total) sad and many people were weeping ... (bitter).

Kapitel 10

A. Text

The Vet

It's the story of a brown bear that ran off. There was a power cut in an amusement centre and the cages didn't lock automatically. The owner and some other persons searched the woods for the bear but they didn't find it. They couldn't trace the escaped animal as there weren't any tracks they could follow as permanent rain had blotted them out. Not finding the bear they telephoned the police station.

The police came in some patrol cars. They looked for the bear until dark began. As night fell they stopped searching for the animal. The next morning they continued the difficult task of finding the bear. They even used a helicopter. Some experts doubted whether such a roaring aircraft would be useful in tracking down the escapee. "The noise will make him nervous and confused and even aggressive", a spokesman said. "And in this season (it was late spring) you won't recognize him", he added.

It was really of no use using the helicopter any longer. Finally a farmer saw his dog barking at the oak-tree near the farmhouse. The farmer came nearer and noticed the bear sleeping on the branches of the tree. Now it was the vet's turn. He took a blowpipe and blew a little dart with a tranquilizer at the bear. (It's a question of the right dosage, you must understand!). The bear was surprised indeed and began groaning. He came down from the tree and began to walk towards the vet. Everybody watched the animal. After a hundred yards the bear was beginning to totter and fell down then.

Four strong men took hold of the corners of a blanket an they carried the sleeping animal (the "furry runaway") back to the amusement centre. The cage was locked carefully and our runaway possibly dreamt of his excursion.

B. Worksheet

I. Answer the questions on the text in complete sentences. If you don't you will lose points.

1. Why could the brown bear run away?
2. What made the search for the bear extremely difficult?
3. Why did they telephone the police?
4. Why did the police stop looking for the bear first?
5. Why were some people against using a helicopter?
6. Why did the season make the search more difficult?
7. Who found the bear finally?
8. Why was it the vet's turn then?
9. Why must the dosage be right?
10. Why did everybody watch the animal?
11. Why is our brown bear called "furry" runaway?
12. Why could he only dream of his excursion?

II. Answer further questions in full sentences as well

1. Say in your own words what a power cut is? Tell me some consequences of such a cut.
2. Describe an amusement centre.
3. Where else is a helicopter used?
4. When are you confused or even aggressive?
5. Do you know persons who used blow pipes as well?
6. When are you surprised?
7. When must you have a blanket?

III. Find synonyms or similar phrases

1. It's a story ...
2. the owner ...
3. ... tracks ...
4. they telephoned ...
5. ... they continued ...
6. ... useful ...
7. ... finally ...
8. ... came nearer ...

9. ... indeed ...
10. everybody ...
11. ... it fell down ...
12. ... excursion ...

IV. The corresponding nouns

1. ... escaped ...
2. ... stopped ...
3. ... difficult
4. ... doubted ...
5. ... confused ...
6. ... aggressive ...
7. ... really ...
8. sleeping ...
9. ... strong ...
10. carefully ...

V. Translation passage

1. Wegen der Blätter konnte man den Bären nicht sehen.
2. Ohne Grund hatten die Bauern Angst um das Vieh, besonders um ihre Kälber, denn der Bär ist Vegetarier.
3. Aber es ist nicht gut, wenn der Bär mit Kindern spielen will, wenn er dich umarmt, wird's gefährlich.
4. "Das ist eine nützliche Information", sagte der Tierarzt.
5. "Können Sie mir weitere Informationen geben", fragte der Wachtmeister.
6. "Ihr alle müßt die Ratschläge der Polizei befolgen."
7. Das ist in der Tat ein guter Rat.
8. "Das ist eine interessante Nachricht", sagte der Wachtmeister zum Bauern.
9. Der Tierarzt setzte seine Brille auf, um die Dosierung besser sehen zu können.
10. Im Vergnügungspark leben viele Tiere in keiner angenehmen Umgebung, sagt die Polizei.

VI. Translation Passage

Give the correct relative pronoun.

1. James Green, der ein guter Tierarzt ist, mag keine Interviews.
2. George Hampton, der den Bären entdeckte, hat wirklich einen schönen Hof.
3. Die Tochter des Tierarztes, die ich gern mag, besucht das Gymnasium.
4. J. G., dessen Praxis etwas altmodisch ist, ist ein guter Tierarzt.
5. Mrs Green, mit der ich auf dem Ball der Feuerwehr tanzte, könnte eine gute Schwiegermutter (!) sein. Ich erinnere Dich an Satz 3!
6. Der Jeep des Tierarztes, der jetzt in der Garage steht, kostete viel.
7. Der Käfig unseres Ausreißers, dessen Gitterstäbe leicht verbogen sind, steht im Zentrum des Vergnügungsparks.
8. Dieser Vergnügungspark, der einem Verein gehört, wird häufig besucht.
9. Diese Cafeteria hier, in der ich gerade sitze, ist eine gute Einrichtung im Freizeitpark.

VII. Translation Passage

Once more the correct relative pronouns. In some cases there are different pronouns possible or you can even leave them out

1. Die Männer, die den Bären trugen, waren Angestellte des Besitzers.
2. Das Mädchen, das ich am Samstag einlud, ist die Tochter des Tierarztes.
3. Die Dame, mit der ich auf dem Feuerwehrball tanzte, ist die Frau des Tierarztes.
4. Das Mädchen, das Leggings trägt, ist ihre Schwester.
5. Aber das Mädchen, an dem ich interessiert bin, ist sie nicht.
6. Der Mann, dessen Hund den Bären fand, ist Bauer.
7. Der Beruf, an dem ich interessiert bin, ist der Beruf des Tierarztes.
8. Das ist ein Beruf, der sehr interessant ist.
9. Das Buch, dessen Inhalt mich faszinierte, war ein Buch über Tiere.
10. Abschließend sage ich, daß die Übersetzung, die Du gerade machst, nicht leicht ist.

VIII. A special exercise on helping verbs or auxiliaries

Find all the synonyms or synonymous phrases with them. Once more a translation passage.

1. Du mußt den Käfig absperren.
2. Er muß (braucht) heute die Ponys nicht zu füttern.
3. Er darf die Ponies nicht reiten.
4. Sie kann den Park besuchen.
5. Wir dürfen in der Cafeteria warten.
6. Ihr solltet nur Mineralwasser trinken.
7. Sie sollten eigentlich (jetzt) die Pferde holen.
8. Ich könnte nicht reiten.
9. Du sollst das Pony bürsten.
10. Gestern sollte der Tierarzt kommen.
11. Der Tierarzt soll eine hübsche Tochter haben.
12. Sie soll morgen heiraten.
13. (Erwartungsgemäß) soll er um 9 kommen.
14. Soll ich gehen?
15. Ich will den Park sehen.

IX. Put Nr. 1, 4, 5, 6, 9, 15 into the negative

X. Make a list of Kap. 10, VIII, Nr. 4

1. present
2. past
3. present perfect
4. past perfect
5. future
6. There is no sense in future perfect!

XI. Shift into past beginning with "Yesterday ..."

1. I must lock the cage every day.
2. You needn't feed the ponies.
3. He can wait there.
4. She can't wait.
5. We may leave the centre.
6. You mustn't enter the cages.

C. Solutions

Kapitel 1

I. Questions on the text

1. You can't do what you want to do. You can't sleep as long as you want to. You can't spend the morning in a pleasant way (pleasantly). You can't drink your cup of coffee slowly. You can't have your breakfast in peace.
2. I dream of the South Sea. I dream of relaxing by the sea. I dream of meeting nice people.
3. I must go to school and work hard. I must learn every day. I must obey my parents.
4. He is dependent as well on a lot of things.
5. It is necessary to make our free time more interesting. Life without work could be boring.
6. My main occupation isn't to kill time. My spare time is very short.

II. Additional Questions

1. I might have got up too late.
2. Usually I go swimming or skiing or I listen to records. A good way of relaxation is playing cards with friends.
3. It consists of green meadows and bushes and hills, blue lakes between the hills, etc.
4. I would read novels and books on history or politics. Or I would read comics or detective stories.
5. I would like to see Italy. There are splendid ancient towns and buildings. There are wonderful vineyards, etc.
6. The state needs money for building and running schools. Roads and motorways must be built.
7. I might worry about spoiled children, unemployment, air pollution, acid rain, social problems, arguments in the family, road accidents, etc.

III. Translate

Diese sogenannten Wunschsätze haben verschiedene "Modelle".

1. I wish I were in the South Sea.
   Du wünschst jetzt, daß Du dort wärest, Du bist aber nicht dort, sondern hier.

Man spricht hier deshalb von einem nicht realen, einem irrealen Wunsch. Die gewünschte Aussage steht in der 1. Vergangenheit **(past).**

2. I wish I hadn't dreamt.
   Hier liegt ein unerfüllter Wunsch der Vergangenheit vor. Die Zeitstufe des ebenfalls irrealen Wunsches ist die 3. Vergangenheit **(past perfect)**.

3. I wish my boss would allow me to take a day off.
   Das ist im Gegensatz zu a) und b) ein realer Wunsch, der möglicherweise erfüllbar ist. Zeitstufe: would + Infinitiv. Beachte, daß **wünschte** hier nicht **wished** sondern **wish** heißt.

   Erfüllbare Wünsche kann man auch mit **want** + Infinitiv ausdrücken.
   Er will sich entspannen. – He wants to relax.
   Vermeide die "herkömmliche" Verwechslung mit **will**:
   He will relax. – Er wird sich entspannen. Zukunft!

Wenn man will, daß jemand etwas tut, braucht man die Konstruktion **want** + Objekt + Infinitiv mit **to.**

Beispiel:

Ich will, daß er arbeitet. *I want him to work.*
Das **daß** wird nicht übersetzt;
aus **he** wird das Objekt **him,**
she wird zu **her**,
they zu **them**!
Zufälligerweise ist die Subjektform eines Hauptworts gleich der Objektform.

Beispiel:

Ich will, daß die Angestellten um 9 Uhr zu arbeiten anfangen.
I want (wish) the employees to start working at 9 o'clock.

IV. Infinitive or -ing-form

1. wearing
2. working
3. to go
4. to earn
5. to work, working

Diese Aufgabe verlangt Kenntnisse, ob der Infinitiv oder die ing-Form genommen wird. Diese **ing**-Form wird auch als Gerund bezeichnet. Sie steht nach bestimmten Verben, z. B. nach

enjoy: genießen, Freude haben an
mind: etwas dagegen haben

Nach anderen Verben ist nur der Infinitiv möglich, z. B. nach:

refuse: sich weigern
manage: zustande bringen, schaffen

"Sonderfälle" erlauben beide Formen, z. B.

start: anfangen
hate: hassen

Im Lehrbuch wirst du sicher eine entsprechende Tabelle finden oder dein Lehrer wird eine Liste ausgeben.

6. getting

   Auch nach einem Hauptwort kann die ing-Form stehen, z. B. nach **problem**, **difficulty**, **fun**.

7. working
8. preparing
9. hearing
10. entweder **proud to be** oder **proud of being**

    Immer wird nach einem Verhältniswort (Präposition), also z. B. nach **of, at, for** oder **in** die **ing**-Form gesetzt. In unserem Fall haben wir die Verbindung

    Eigenschaftswort = Adjektiv + Verhältniswort = Adjektiv + ing-Form.

    Sonderfälle auch hier: Bei einigen Adjektiven kann auch die Infinitivkonstruktion "angehängt" werden, z. B. **to be proud to be**. Eine "Vermischung" der beiden Formen ist zu vermeiden. Also klar unterscheiden!

    Sie fürchtet sich (davor), im Meer zu schwimmen.
    She is afraid of swimming in the sea, so ...
    She is afraid to swim in the sea, but she has to.

11. living
12. getting
13. working

    Entsprechend muß auf ein Verb + Verhältniswort die ing-Form folgen. Übrigens ist das **to** in der Frage 13 kein Infinitiv-to!

14. going
15. Auch nach Hauptwort + Verhältniswort wird die **ing**-Form gesetzt. marrying, becoming, marrying
16. Diesmal wird die Grammatik durch eine Übersetzung "abgefragt".
    a) As soon as Mr Flisher saw the daughter he wanted to marry her.
    Oder: On seeing the daughter Mr Flisher wanted to marry her.
    Präge dir also ein, daß **sobald, als** zwei Varianten hat.
    b) Mr Clever worked for 20 years without paying taxes.
    c) After the tax office had found it out, he had to pay 5651.05 GBP.
    Oder: After finding (it) out the tax office forced Mr Clever to pay 5651.05 GBP.
    Nach dem Verhältniswort, teilweise auch nach dem Bindewort, z. B. **after** oder **before,** muß also die **ing**-Form stehen.
    Natürlich setzt man auch nach jedem Verhältniswort in beliebigen Verbindungen die **ing**-Form, z. B. nach
    apart from: abgesehen von,
    instead of: anstatt.

> **Beispiel:**
> Abgesehen davon, daß er erschöpft war, war er ganz zufrieden.
> *Apart from being tired out he was quite satisfied.*

V. Put in the correct tense of the words given in brackets

1. gave
2. will buy
3. want
4. were
5. learnt
6. wouldn't have started
7. will dress
8. were invited
9. had had; had been given;

Diese sogenannten Bedingungssätze sind dir auch als **if-clauses** geläufig, da das Bindewort **if** (falls, wenn) das entscheidende Wort ist. **Unless = if not.** Grundsätzlich unterscheidet man drei Muster:

a) **if**-Satz Gegenwart, Hauptsatz Zukunft. Übungssatz 2, 7; Nr. 3 gehört als Sonderform auch hierher: **if**-Satz Gegenwart, Hauptsatz mit Hilfszeitwort auch Gegenwart. Im Hauptsatz des 1. Musters können also stehen **must**, **can**, **may** und eben auch **will** als Zukunftsanzeiger!

b) **if**-Satz 1. Vergangenheit, Hauptsatz 1. Bedingungsform **(conditional)**. Dieses 2. Muster findet man im Übungssatz 1 und 8. Sonderformen sind die Übungssätze 4 und 5.

c) **if**-Satz 3. Vergangenheit, Hauptsatz 2. Bedingungsform (**perfect conditional**); Übungssätze 6 und 9. In diesem 3. Muster könnte auch **might have** und **could have** vorkommen.

10. will be bought
11. had been sent
12. was (were) given (Nrn. 8, z. T. 9, 10, 11 und 12 sind Passivkonstruktionen; vgl. dazu Kap. 7, V und VI).

VI. Ask the questions

Auch in einer höheren Jahrgangsstufe muß die Fragebildung geprüft werden, da häufig immer noch Fehler der unteren Klassen vorkommen, und gerade auch in der Abschlußprüfung die korrekte Form der Fragebildung verlangt wird.

1. Did you have to get up early?
   Have to = must = müssen; **had to** = 1. Vergangenheit = **past**. Diese Phrase muß immer mit **do, does, did** "umschrieben" werden. Nochmals ein Satz in der Gegenwart:
   a) Must he work?
   b) Does he have to work?
   Has he to work oder *Have they to work* ist **falsch**!

2. Does he brush?

3. Did he have eggs ...?
   Wenn **have** die Bedeutung **einnehmen, essen** hat, muß "umschrieben" werden.
   Die gleiche Regel gilt auch bei *"Do we have English?"*

Kapitel 2

I. Answer the questions on the text in complete sentences

1. In the trailer there was a machine which produced electricity.
2. The pupils saw their first film.
3. In the classroom of 1950 there was only a blackboard, there wasn't any technical equipment.
4. They were able to learn English in a language lab (oratory).
5. The pupil can hear whether his answer is correct ... whether his pronunciation is correct.
6. The equipment was new ... modern.
7. "Mr Hedgehog" began to run while "Mrs Hedgehog" was just waiting at the finish line.
8. He thinks that some day the present computers will be out of date like the language labs which were totally old-fashioned like the huge recorders.
9. No, he doubts it.
10. Computers are a vital part of life, industry and business.
11. You can either make programmes or you simply learn (how) to write texts.

II. Answer further questions in full sentences as well

1. Pupils have been accustomed to these new "machines" as modern playthings. Younger persons can handle new technical things more easily than grown-ups.
2. They might think their children have better job opportunities.
3. In almost every job or profession I must work with computers.
4. a) The fox and the grapes
   b) The lion, the fox and the ass
   c) The fox and the goose
5. a) I must have skis, ski sticks, a ski suit, a ski cap or helmet,
   b) I must have a rope, a helmet, special waterproof clothing, a torch, hooks and a hammer ...
   c) It depends on the subjects of a day ... a satchel, a pencil case, pens, several textbooks, exercise-books, copy-books ...
6. No they can't see Lord Horatio Nelson. He died in 1805. We can merely see an actor.

7. The pupils had to write test papers. They didn't like that as they couldn't copy from their neighbour ... crib off their neighbour ...
8. Dinosaurs died out a long time ago. There aren't dinosaurs any more. The computers of 1992 might be dinosaurs after a time and "die out" as well.

III. Fill in synonyms

1. been accustomed
2. must look at, must notice
3. an extraordinarily
4. In the beginning, originally
5. make the children able, make it possible for the children to ...
6. part
7. Despite the ... must ...
8. fear

IV. Complete the sentences

1. us to use
2. them to buy
3. her to deal
4. for you to learn
5. for everybody to become
6. ... clever of them to learn

Zu Nr. 1, 2 und 3 siehe Lösungshinweise Kap. 1, III unten.
Zu Nr. 4 und 5:

wichtig für ... **important for** + Objekt + Infinitiv.

Hierher gehören auch:

useful for, possible for, necessary for ...

Zu Nr. 6:

klug von ... **clever of** + Objekt + Infinitiv.

Weitere Beispiele für diese Konstruktion:

tactful of, kind of, silly of ...

Vergleiche auch Lösungshinweise Kap. 1, IV.

V. Complete once more. Insert the correct preposition

1. ... the author for telling ...
2. ... to working hard ...
3. ... from playing ...

Beachte die Konstruktion Verb + Verhältniswort + **-ing**-Form. Das **to** in Nr. 2 ist ein Verhältniswort, kein Infinitiv (siehe auch Kap. 1, IV).

VI. The correct tense

1. wouldn't have seen ...
2. had known
3. presses
4. will use
5. was ill (were ill)
6. will (would)

Siehe auch Kap. 1, V, sowohl Aufgaben als auch Lösungshinweise.
Nr. 6 ist eine "Sonderform".

VII. The correct tense

1. began
2. has seen
3. have been
4. will attend
5 had bought
6. was working

Vergleiche auch Aufgaben und Lösungshinweise Kap. 5, III, Kap. 7, III und Kap. 7, IV.

VIII. Ask your friend

1. Do you want to have a try?
   Are you willing to ...
   Do you wish to ...
   Do you intend to ...
   Vergleiche Kap. 10, VIII, 15.
2. Is school influenced by the computers?
   Vergleiche Kap. 8, III.

3. Must we adopt ... accept ... the new technology?
   Do we have to ...
   Are we forced to ...
   Are we compelled to ...
   Are we obliged to ...
   Vergleiche Kap. 10, VIII–XI.
4. Who supplies us with software?
   Who is supplying us ...

IX. Definitions

1. All the things which are necessary for any purpose ...
   All the things which (that) you need for anything.
2. A small motor vehicle (car) with four-wheel drive. Usually it has got a folding top. When you take away the top you will have a cabriolet.
3. It's a story in which animals or plants and things speak. A fable teaches us a moral or lesson.
4. It has spines. It can roll itself into a ball to defend itself.
5. It's your job, vocation or profession you have been trained for.
6. A big reptile which lived long, long ago but has died out.
7. It's a radical political change or a total change of living (conditions).
8. It's a sort of music where a lot of drums are beaten.
9. A lawyer helps people in a trial ... in a court ...
10. A person who makes contracts. You need him when you want to sell your house.
11. It's a big shop with many departments.
12. It's the room where the doctor treats a patient ... where a patient is examined.
13. a) You can leave a prison, a camp ...
    b) You interrupt a computer activity.
    c) You leave a function of a computer menu and choose another function.

X. Find the opposite

1. to increase, to make bigger
2. modern, in
3. begin, start, commence
4. disconnect, separate, cut in two
5. went away, left
6. private

XI. Complete the list

1. attention, attentive
2. sight
3. technique, technology, technician
4. produce, product; productive
5. poverty
6. connection
7. number, numerous
8. belief, believable
9. enthusiastic
10. existence, existing
11. excitement, excite

XII. A minister was talking about computer technology. Some journalists wrote down what he said. Start with:

The minister said (asked) ...

1. The minister said that several years before only specalists knew (had known) to deal ...
2. He said that the day before he visited (had visited) children ... who had to use (had been forced to use ...)
   Vergleiche Kap. 5, IV; Kap. 6, IV; Kap. 10, VIII.
3. He said that for many years he had been a fan ... would finance ...
4. ... that everybody had to support (was compelled to support ...)
   Vergleiche Kap. 5, IV; Kap. 6, IV; Kap. 10, VIII.
5. ... that you weren't forced to give up ... you didn't have to give up ... as they were ... (had been) before ...
6. He asked whether (if) we (you, they) believed that ... would be ... following decade.
7. He asked when we would publish what he had said ...
   Vergleiche Kap. 5, IV; Kap. 6, IV.

Kapitel 3

I. Questions on the text

1. They think it hasn't got anything to do with (European) culture.
2. They use plastic dishes and boxes. They think that you eat too quickly there.
3. I think the parents aren't accustomed to that sort of restaurant.
4. They ought to abolish plastic plates and cups and boxes.
5. He was in charge of the navy.
6. Gambling was his hobby, his favourite activity.
7. No, I can't see it from the text.
8. He was just gambling and didn't have time for lunch or dinner so he simply ate "fast food".
9. It might be a true statement.
10. An "original" sandwich is two slices of bread with roast beef in between, a French baguette is a loaf of white bread with ham and cheese and some lettuce leaves and slices of cucumber.
11. It is the best, it is consumed everywhere, it might be the best-selling of them all.
12. "Oh, super, great, let's go in, it's really exciting."
13. He was a nobleman and he wasn't compelled to help himself. There were a lot of staff who cared for the earl and minister. I find waiters and waitresses in restaurants and cafes.

II. Additional Questions

1. I think it's culture as it is a product of people's minds and many artists created it. On the other hand it's kitsch as it's only imitation and rather silly. On the one hand it may be necessary as it provides spare time activities especially for kids, on the other hand there are many other facilities somewhere for the kids. The advantages are that there are many forms of entertainment in one center. I think a great disadvantage is that kids might believe culture is concentrated in this "mini world".
2. I can fill a sandwich with pork, schnitzel, slices of any sausage, cucumber, etc.
3. They can see what they want to eat, they needn't wait, it's "modern", chips and coke are favourized by kids, they can sit where they like or even stand (Grown-ups think they're younger!)

4. They say it isn't good for your health. You must spend a longer time and not only devour your food. And they don't accept the plastic containers.
5. It's rather cheap. You needn't pay for the service. You needn't pay any tips to the waiter or waitress. It doesn't take a long time (if you are in a hurry). Most fast-food restaurants are very clean and the staff is very neat. The food is appetizing and inviting.
6. In a fast-food restaurant you collect your food and put it on a tray. You can sit. At a snack-bar or kiosk you order your meal and you usually have to stand. There the choice mightn't be so big.
7. It's like a ceremony as it has got many parts (or courses) beginning with the starters, the main course and the dessert accompanied by the proper wine.
8. You must gamble, you can't stop doing it. You can be addicted to alcohol, smoking, drugs. In some cases you can be addicted to work as a "workaholic". You can help those people if you don't drink any alcohol when your friend is an alcoholic or the addicts must be sent to special hospitals for special treatment or cures.
9. A sandwich is two slices of bread with meat or something else between them; a baguette is a "French" loaf of white bread "filled" with bacon and green salad or something else; a hamburger is a bread roll with minced beef, lettuce and slices of onion.
10. A snob sandwich might be a sandwich with lobster, shrimps, prawns.
11. People who don't have time or are in a hurry or think eating anything needn't be "celebrated".
12. A menu in a restaurant is a list of the dishes. The menu on the computer screen shows the different functions of the computer.
13. A recipe tells you how to cook or bake something. The doctor gives you a presciption of the medicine you can buy at the drugstore or chemist's.
14. They think meat isn't good for the body and you can live longer if you only eat vegetables, eggs or mushrooms.
15. They don't drink alcohol or eat too much food.

III. Definitions

1. Culture is everything that the human mind has created and is more than civilisation: art, music, beliefs, literature, science, etc. Civilisation might be a part of culture.
2. It's a big entertainment centre where you can amuse yourself.
3. Chips are fried potato strips.
4. Member of a government
5. playing games for money
6. a sort of nobleman
7. the meat of an ox, cow
8. It's an animal out of the sea with a hard shell, a crustacian.
9. Things you need when you cook or bake, or the parts of a recipe.

IV. Agree

1. "So it is."
2. "I don't either.", "Neither do I."
3. "So was I.", "I was(,) too."
4. "So did I.", " I did(,) too."

Vergleiche Kap. 1, VII.

V. Mixed Grammar Passage: Now we are leaving fast-food-restaurants and are talking about Paul Bocuse, the famous chef:

1. would be
2. would have become, of getting
3. really, being, to help
4. have studied, usually
5. found, delicious
6. hasn't been answered
7. of garnishing
8. leaves
9. (in) doing
10. tasted, extraordinarily excellent, wholly
11. most charming, in a friendly way
12. most elegant
13. laying
14. mechanically

15. extremely carefully
16. has been broken

Zu den Umstandsangaben vgl. Lösungshinweise Kap. 6, VII und Kap. 9, VI..

VI. Now we aren't filling our sandwiches, we have to fill in the same or similar expressions in the gaps:

1. tolerate
2. have a rest
3. actually
4. likes
5. wonder (ohne **themselves**)
6. kind
7. get angry
8. plain
9. modern, like ... better
10. a small number of, brave
11. ungenerous
12. quickly
13. think, oughtn't to
14. much
15. typical
16. occasionally
17. go on
18. best-known
19 made

Vergleiche Kap. 2, III und Kap. 10, III.

Kapitel 4

I. Questions on the text

1. He didn't spend (his) money ... hasn't spent (his) money on going out and he didn't buy elegant suits.
2. He learnt the trade of (an) insurance.
3. Yes, indeed. Apart from being slim she wore black leggings and mini skirts.
4. a) He didn't own a car.
   b) And he wanted to go dancing in the neighbouring town. (You must understand they couldn't walk or go by bicycle, the girl sitting on the luggage carrier!)
5. The blocks of flats collapse, bridges fall into the rivers, there are huge gaps or splits in the roads, the earthquake causes gas explosions as the gas tubes break, it causes fire, the electricity is cut. People are killed and injured, or slain or buried under the ruins. Note: In our region earthquakes haven't been so bad up to now.
6. Persons who suffer from heart diseases. In addition: Aged people who can't escape quickly, also handicapped or paralysed ones. (Persons who live in tall blocks of flats.)
7. The region might be radioactively contaminated if the plant is destroyed or the nuclear reactor is damaged.
8. He was in a bad mood as the car he had borrowed from his brother was damaged. Fair's mood wasn't better, as it was his car.
9. He had taken out an insurance against earthquakes. It was a wise plan indeed!
10. It was the apprentice's first contract and it was a very good idea in fact. The apprentice succeeded in making a contract all by himself.
11. Possibly. He may get married to Monica some years later. But things too often change as feelings change as well.
12. He only listened to the radio and didn't see the actual destruction caused by the earthquake.
13. People needed help. They wanted to know what was going on.
14. The top ... the roof or the windscreen was damaged.
15. The roof (a lot of dents!) and the windscreen had to be replaced.

II. Additional Questions

1. I can insure myself against accidents, theft, fire, injuries.
2. She must have fair (dark) hair, she must be slim, elegantly dressed. She must be friendly, helpful, faithful. He: tall, his favourite clothing denim jeans, must be sporty and active, should not brag and flatter, etc.
3. He or she doesn't like the bad qualities of the partner any longer. He or she has another partner who is far more interesting and charming (indeed!).
4. They might dance there or simply meet other young people or they like the music.
5. I must be helped after an accident or if the car has broken down.
6. An insurance against theft: Car thefts are not unusual today. Your new car cost a lot of money and is no longer there ... has vanished.
7. There are several ways of attracting the other sex: Clothing, your eyes, the way you speak, a two-seater. Be handsome, etc.
8. There are numerous tricks. I'd say you simply start a conversation in an amusing way. A witty small talk is even better than asking whether you saw the girl on TV the day before.
9. It's not unusual but try to find another (a better) partner. Any separation is painful I know but the pain will lessen and stop.
10. Has he got a driving-licence?
11. There are accidents and incidents. A life insurance policy can prevent you from having problems when you are aged.
12. Psychologists say the person reminds you of some nice person you had to do with before.
13. We need cars
    a) for going to work,
    b) for going shopping
    c) for spending our spare time,
    d) for being independent and mobile.

III. Definitions

Natürlich sind auch andere Definitionen möglich. Benutze das Wörterbuch!

1. It's the town where you were born and have been living since then.
2. An apprentice learns the skills of a trade or business or any handicraft (usually for a longer period of time).

3. An insurance company is a sort of firm which deals with insurances or life insurances; it makes contracts and helps you after an accident by paying the insurance (money).
4. It's a rather short skirt.
5. In an earthquake the earth is shaken heavily (in these parts only slightly).
6. Panic is a very big and uncontrolled fear where you can't use your mind any longer.
7. A hospital is a building where doctors and nurses work and patients are examined, treated and operated on and stay there for a longer time.
8. The doctor puts penicillin into your body by a needle (syringe).
9. It's the contract with an insurance company which says how much you must pay a month or a year and how much you can get in the case of an accident or theft.

Vergleiche Kap. 2, IX, und Kap. 3, III.

IV. Infinitive or -ing-form

Das ist ein schwieriger Grammatikbereich. Im Lehrbuch findet man sicher entsprechende Tabellen. Der "wirtschaftlich" denkende Schüler lernt gegebenenfalls nur die Tabelle mit den **ing**-Formen. Aber es gilt auch hier: **Learning by practising or simply by seeing**. Siehe auch Kap. 1, IV.

1. being
2. to invite
3. giving
4. to win
5. to pay
6. dancing
7. being
8. to dance
9. going; to go
10. being; to be.

V. Decide whether you take oneself or one another: There is no emphatic use.

Der Hinweis **no emphatic use** will sagen, daß es sich um die Entsprechung von **sich** handelt (sonst dürfte man ja die Form von **oneself** immer verwenden (vgl. auch Kap. 4, VI und Kap. 4, VIII sowie Kap. 4, VII).

1. himself
2. –
3. (yourself)
4. to one another (to each other)
5 –
6. –
7. each other (one another)
8. themselves
9. –

VI. Übersetzungspassage

Gerade durch eine Übersetzung werden Grammatikbereiche eingeübt und abgefragt, die in bloßen Einsetzungsübungen eher als "Glückstreffer" erscheinen.

1. Did the young people enjoy themselves? (Did the young people amuse themselves in the disco?) (1. Vergangenheit!)
2. I didn't introduce myself to Monica.
3. Did she adapt herself to him?
4. Did you have to change? Were you forced to change? Were you compelled to change? Were you obliged to change?
   Hier hast Du alle "Ersatzformen" für **must** in der 1. Vergangenheit; Vergleiche Kap. 10, VIII–XI. **change** erlaubt kein Reflexivpronomen)
5. Do you remember the first kiss? (kein Reflexivpronomen!)
6. We were not interested in the others; (kein Reflexivpronomen!)
7. Aren't you glad about the date? (kein R.)
8. For two years he has taken care of her. (... has been taking care of her).
   a) kein R.
   b) **seit** + Zeitraum = **for**
   c) auch die Verlaufsform ist natürlich möglich, siehe Kap. 7, III.
9. Does she take it upon herself to stand his bad qualities?
10. When must we say goodbye? When do we have to say goodbye?
    Vergleiche auch Kap. 4, V.

VII. Eine weitere Übersetzungspassage

Im Grunde genommen kann die entsprechende Form von **oneself** immer genommen werden, wenn es sich um ein **betonendes Fürwort** oder **emphasizing pronoun** handelt, also entsprechend **selbst, selber**. Verstärkungen sind **all by oneself**. Ist es "bloß" ein **Reflexivpronomen**, dann ist es nicht immer erlaubt (vgl. Lösungen Kap. 4, V und VI).

1. You can't repair the car yourself (all by yourself).
2. He drove the car into the garage himself (all by himself)
3. The boss was interested in the car **himself** (vgl. oben Kap. 4, VI, 6.).
4. Did he make a mistake? (Kein Reflexivpronomen!).
5. The driver was angry. (kein R.)
6. "I can apologize myself", he said. (Vergleiche damit: Er entschuldigt sich. He apologizes).
7. The car approached (all) by itself as the brakes were out of order. (Vergleiche: Der Mann näherte sich. The man approached).
8. The driver apologized (vgl. Nr. 6.).
9. He was angry himself. (Er ärgerte sich: He was angry).
10. The incident (story) happened yesterday (kein Reflexivpronomen!).

VIII. Translation passage

Hier geht es um das wechselseitige Fürwort oder **reciprocal pronoun**. Nicht nach jedem Verb darf man es anfügen, wie du gleich sehen wirst.

1. Monica and I couldn't meet for a long time.
2. But then we met every day.
3. We kissed heartily and looked at each other tenderly.
4. We never quarrelled.
5. We wondered (asked ourselves) why other couples parted.
6. "Do you get along with each other"? our friends asked.
7. After a short time we became engaged and got married.
8. At the wedding reception the relatives introduced themselves to one another;

   each other wird gewöhnlich bei **zwei** Personen gebraucht; hier haben wir auch ein Reflexivpronomen.
9. We always want to talk to each other even when it's hard.
10. If they help each other they won't get divorced.

    Ein kleiner Hinweis: Sachverhalte, die mit Liebe zu tun haben, "verbieten" das wechselseitige Fürwort, weil ja Liebe ohnehin wechselseitig ist.

    Aber: They loved each other (one another).

Kapitel 5

I. Answer the questions on the text in complete sentences:

1. He had to work hard and his brother-in-law had visited him.
2. Yes, he was. His wife wasn't at home as she was meeting her classmates.
3. He thought somebody had broken the window panes.
4. He was informed when his wife came home and told him about the containers.
5 It was a council site.
6. The people who throw in bottles after 8 p.m. cause a lot of trouble.
7. There were piles of newspapers outside the containers. In our man's garden there were newspapers, too.

II. Answer the additional questions in full sentences as well:

1. He talks a lot about boring things, drinks a lot or he doesn't say anything at all.
2. It's the book you like best. You read the book as often as you can.
3. I must do so, so that nobody enters the house.
4. There was a sticker to say when it was forbidden to throw in bottles.
5. I don't throw away things or boxes in the street,
   I don't pour poisonous waste into the waste pipe,
   I don't put used batteries into the litter box,
   I don't put used things which can be recycled in the dustbin (garbage can),
   I use different containers for my rubbish ...
6. The best idea can be spoilt by reckless people who don't obey the regulations.

III. Put in the correct tense of the word in brackets:

1. Bei diesem Signalwort ist klar:
   visited
2. is living.
   Hier ist die ursprüngliche Bedeutung der Verlaufsform **(continuous form, progressive form)** gemeint: **jetzt**.
3. Singgemäß **bis jetzt**, also 2. Vergangenheit (**present perfect**):
   has met; **since** verlangt diese Zeit.
   Auch: has been meeting.

Die Verlaufsform setzt sich immer mehr durch und hat auch den Sinn einer ununterbrochenen Handlung, oder sie will etwas betonen bzw. herausstellen (vgl. Hinweise Kap. 7, III).

4. was: 1960 – 1972!
   had been: **after** bedeutet die Vorzeitigkeit; die Vorzeitigkeit der 1. Vergangenheit **(past)** ist die 3. Vergangenheit **(past perfect)**.
5. have been:
   For (seit, gemeint ist auch **bis jetzt)** verlangt die 2. Vergangenheit. **(present perfect;** vgl. oben Frage 3).
6. will have built, (will) have constructed: **by (bis)**.
   Bis zu einem bestimmten Zeitpunkt der Zukunft wird eine Tätigkeit oder Handlung abgeschlossen sein: 2. Zukunft **(future perfect)**.
7. will:
   Next month signalisiert Zukunft.
8. a) Angenommen **usually** + Gegenwart, also **puts**, dann **has realised;** die Vorzeitigkeit der Gegenwart **(present)** ist die 2. Vergangenheit **(present perfect)**.
   b) Angenommen **usually** + 1. Vergangenheit., also **put**, dann **had realised;**
   die Vorzeitigkeit der 1. Vergangenheit ist die 3. Vergangenheit **(past perfect**; vgl. Frage 4).
9. was doing so:
   Wenn in eine Handlung jemand oder etwas "hineinplatzt" **(I addressed)**, nimmt man für erstere die Verlaufsform **(continuous form, progressive form;** vgl. Kapitel 7, IV, 11).
10. He lost his temper as he loses:
    Die Handlung spielt noch in der 1. Vergangenheit **(past)**, was aber grundsätzlich geschieht (typisch ist), steht in der Gegenwart **(present**; vgl. Kap. 2, VII; Kap. 7, III; Kap. 7, IV.)

IV. Write down what the mayor said the day before

Die direkte Rede verlangt genaue Kenntnisse über:
a) die notwendige Zeitstufe und
b) die Bildung dieser Zeitstufe selbst (gerade beim Hilfszeitwort).

Steht das berichtende Verb in der 1. Vergangenheit, 3. Vergangenheit oder Bedingungsform, muß die Zeit bei der Umformung der direkten in die indirekte Rede "verschoben" werden.

	direkte Rede	indirekte Rede
a)	Gegenwart	1. Vergangenheit
b)	1. Vergangenheit	1. Vergangenheit oder 3. Vergangenheit
c)	2. Vergangenheit	3. Vergangenheit
d)	3. Vergangenheit	3. Vergangenheit
e)	1. Zukunft	1. Bedingungsform
f)	2. Zukunft	2. Bedingungsform
g)	1. Bedingungsform	2. Bedingungsform oder 1. Bedingungsform
h)	2. Bedingungsform	2. Bedingungsform

Beispiele: to like – to be

	direkte Rede		indirekte Rede	
a)	He said:	"I like."	(that)	... he liked.
b)		"I liked."	(that)	... he liked. ... he had liked.
c)		"I have liked."	(that)	... he had liked.
d)		"I had liked."	(that)	... he had liked.
e)		"I will like."	(that)	... he would like
f)		"I will have liked."	(that)	... he would have liked.
g)		"I would like."	(that)	... he would have liked ... he would like.
h)		"I would have liked."	(that)	... he would have liked.

	direkte Rede		indirekte Rede	
a)	He said:	"I am ..."	(that)	... he was
b)		"I was ...	(that)	... he was; ... he had been
c)		"I have been ...	(that)	... he had been.
d)		"I had been ..."	(that)	... he had been.
e)		"I will be ..."	(that)	... he would be
f)		"I would have been ..."	(that)	... he would have been.
g)		"I would be ..."	(that)	... he would have been ... he would be.
h)		"I would have been ..."	(that)	... he would have been.

(vgl. auch Kap. 2, XII; Kap. 6, IV; Kap. 7, III und IV; Kap. 7, V und VI)

Das Hilfszeitwort muß ebenfalls verschoben werden. Das geschieht durch die Ersatzformen (vgl. Kap. 10, VIII–XI). Das direkte **can, may, shall** kann auch zum indirekten **could, might, should** umgeformt werden. Das direkte **should, could, might, ought to** verändert sich indirekt nicht. Beachte auch die veränderte Person und die abzuändernden besitzanzeigenden Pronomen:

He said, "I hate my car."
He said that **he** hated **his** car.

Vergiß auch nicht, die Zeitangaben u. ä. zu verändern (siehe die entsprechenden Lösungen)!

Hinweis:
Steht das berichtende Verb in der Gegenwart, Zukunft oder 2. Vergangenheit, ändert sich "indirekt" die Zeit nicht.

Beispiel:
He always says, "I hate my car."
He always says that he hates his car.

The mayor said (that) ...

1. we (they, you) were keen ...
2. there was ... which forbade
3. the following (next) day there would be ...
4. we (they, you) had to (were forced to, were compelled to, were obliged to) use ...
5. we (they, you) weren't allowed (permitted) to use ...
6. could (were able to, were allowed to) make ... (vgl. Kap. 10, VIII–XI)
7. ... environment was ...
8. that had been ... up to then.
9. ... of that he didn't like those ... only ate ...
10. the year before he visited (had visited) an ...
11. ...we (they, you) would have ...
12. we (they, you) might (could, were allowed to, were permitted to) use our (their, your) resources but we (they, you) had to (were forced to, were obliged to, were compelled to) use ...
13. they should ...
14. ... had realised ... they changed (had changed) their minds.
15. then he was going to welcome his ... from our (their, your) twin ... (vgl. auch Kap. 2, XII und Kap. 6, IV).

Kapitel 6

I. Questions on the text

1. They were friendlier as there was a park around the grey building.
2. Everybody liked him and regarded him as a member of the class, as fellow pupil, as classmate.
3. No he wasn't, he was even unfair.
4. He simply wanted to teach the pupil who was able to command and who had to obey. He intended to make clear to him that in his gym lessons everybody had to do what he told them to do.
5. The pupil didn't like the teacher or P. E. either.
6. The inner connection was that Max rejected the gym teacher and therefore sport as well.
7. I can't imagine that at all as the teacher wasn't kind, he was too strict.
8. The P. E. teacher was ill.
9. It's vital to relax our muscles in order to be fit for the match. (You must warm up.)
10. The pupils were too far away from the teacher.
11. He wasn't wearing running shoes.
12. Usually the teacher speaks more than a pupil in the classroom. They may have been a bit shy.

II. Additional questions

1. They want to start a new career. Persons are transferred from one place to another (civil servants, officers).
2. a) I stop attending that school.
   b) I finish working there.
   c) I say goodbye.
3. It's an artificial garden with trees and benches where I can relax. I can sit on a bench, walk, lie on the lawn (if permitted).
4. They stand for physical education.
5. He simply wasn't a fan of P. E.
6. You are sent to hospital after an accident, after an injury, when you must be operated on, mothers-to-be (expectant mothers) are taken to hospital as well.
7. The surgeon enabled him.
8. He was handicapped for many weeks.

9. Max would have been handicapped for the rest of his life. The operation would have failed.
10. I can take flowers, books, radio cassettes, magazines.
11. Personal answers: I would have more (fewer) lessons. The opponents think that other subjects are more important for your future career. The correct spelling (orthography) is more vital than playing volleyball.
12. They could be avoidable if the teacher and the pupils minded the dangers. Young kids usually are enthusiastic and aren't aware of the dangers.
13. It might be a special science. Think of the top athletes or sportsmen (sportswomen). There is a team of physicists, mathematicians, food chemists and vitamin experts who are in charge of the (Olympic) competitors.

III. Further questions

1. They get gold, silver and bronze medals. They don't only get gold they also get glory for their country which is therefore a nation of sport.
2. The Olympic flame comes from Olympia in Greece where the original Olympic Games were held.

IV. Write down what the reporter said. Start with:

The reporter said (that) ...

1. a burning arrow lit (had lit) the Olympic flame
2. the XXV Summer Olympics were (had been) opened by ...
3. more than 170 national teems would take ...
4. some nations returned (had returned) as they were (had been) absent
5. some teams thought they could (were able to) use the games to get ...
6. they had replaced ...
7. the organizers emphasized that ... had to be forbidden
8. that sort ... wasn't allowed to be accepted
9. that year everybody ... looked confident
10. then he was talking to ... who had arrived there the day before
11. had been ... up to then
12. he would write ... the following year (the year to come).

Vergleiche Kap. 2, XII und Kap. 5, IV.

V. Say in a different way using the ing-form

1. On hearing ...
2. While sitting ...
3. After having won ... (after winning; having won)
4. Before doing ...
5. Since wearing a T-shirt ... the runner is heartily .. (vgl. Frage 9).
6. If invited (hier liegt das Mittelwort der Vergangenheit, **past participle,** im Passivsinn vor!)
7. When arriving ...
8. After having run ... (vgl. oben Nr. 3)
9. Being a fast swimmer, Mr Biondi is always surrounded ... (In diesem Fall muß ich den Namen nochmal aufgreifen, sonst geht er "verloren".)
10. Not liking publicity she ...
    Grundsätzlich folgt auf das Verhältniswort, die Präposition, **the preposition,** das Mittelwort. Je nach Sinn taucht es als **present participle (sitting)** oder als **past participle (invited)** auf (vgl. Kap. 1, IV).

VI. Translate

1. Apart from making some slight faults she can hope to get a medal.
2. In spite of fearing (being afraid of) slight mishaps she is optimistic.
3. Instead of hanging around in cafeterias our reporter is watching each event.
4. She talked about it without blushing.
5. She hopes to win by wearing a tight swimsuit.
6. In (for) examining many athletes he got the name "doping inspector".

Vergleiche Kap. 1, IV und Kap. 6, V.

VII. Mixed Grammar Passage

1. ... extraordinarily fast
   (Wie schnell? Man nennt diese Umstandsangabe eine des Grads, der Intensität, **adverb of degree**; **fast** ohne **-ly**).
2. ... used to running (**-ing** nach Verhältniswort) ... has been fond (bis jetzt: **present peerfect**).
3. silly (nach **sound**, **look**, **taste**, **smell**, **seem** u. a. kein **-ly**; vgl. "He behaves sillily) ... completely ... slowly
   (Diese Umstandsangabe heißt Umstandsangabe der Art und Weise, **adverb of manner**).

4. ... has been (siehe Frage 2) ... walking (to walk).
5. ... particularly (siehe Frage 1) ... good (siehe Frage 3) ... seeing (siehe Frage 2).
6. ... occasionally ... frequently
(Diese Umstandsangaben werden als Umstandsangaben der Häufigkeit, **adverbs of frequency,** bezeichnet).
7. Naturally ... hard (auch **hard** ohne **-ly**).
8. ... winning
(siehe Frage 2; vgl. auch Kap. 1, III: Objekt und Infinitiv: We can rely on her to win.)
9. ... taking ... getting (siehe Frage 2).
10. ... more quickly
(immer diese Form der Steigerung, außer Ausnahmen, siehe Frage 11).
11. ... better (vgl. **worse**)
12. ... extremely well
(vgl. Frage 1; **well** ist die Umstandsangabe von good).
13. ...(e)specially ethusiastically
(Eigenschaftswort, Adjektiv, **adjective** auf **-ic** fügt in der Umstandsangabe **-ally** an; vgl. auch Kap. 3, V und Kap. 9, VI.)

Kapitel 7

I. Answer the questions on the text in complete sentences

1. The environment (nature) ist damaged (endangered) by exhaust fumes and other exhaust gases.
2. You have to pay less.
3. Travelling is cheaper and people earn more money.
4. They leave rubbish (waste) behind.
5. There are fast-food stalls and souvenir shops as well as traders.
6. They don't get seats in restaurants and tourists overcrowd the towns. (They don't like half-naked tourists.)
7. As well as the requirements of the environment those of tourism must be fulfilled.
8. People breathing and sweating in them damage the buildings.

II. Answer the additional questions in full sentences as well

1. I can walk or cycle if possible. I don't go faster than x miles (y kilometres) p. h. (Many other answers possible).
2. The state wants the car drivers not to go by car so often (to use public means of transport instead if there are any).
3. They are in the summer holidays.
4. They have to gather hankies, newspapers, paper bags, etc.
5. When you are in a foreign country you must pay attention to the habits and practices there.
6. I reject their behaviour as they are guests. I think it's not aesthetic when you aren't dressed properly, there is a lack of the sense of beauty.
7. The journeys must cost more, the numbers of tourists must be limited, we must prevent pollution by severe fines, tourists must be convinced that not everything they like to do can be done, what we need ist **eco**-tourism which harmonizes with (the) **eco**logy.

III. Make a list of both simple form and progressive form (continuous form), active

1. a) She travels
   b) She is travelling
2. a) She travelled
   b) She was travelling

3. a) She has travelled
   b) She has been travelling
4. a) She had travelled
   b) She had been travelling
5. a) She will travel
   b) She will be travelling (auf andere einfache Zukunftsformen wird hingeweisen: She is going to leave. She is leaving),
6. a) She will have travelled
   b) She will have been travelling
7. a) She would travel
   b) She would be travelling
8. a) She would have travelled
   b) She would have been travelling.

Die einfache Form (simple form) meint mehr die Tatsache (the fact): He smokes: Er raucht, er ist (ein) Raucher. Die sogenannte Verlaufsform (continuous form, progressive form) bedeutet:

- etwas geschieht gerade;
- man will anschaulich darstellen;
- ein Vorgang wird nicht unterbrochen;
- in ein Geschehen kommt von "außen" eine Unterbrechung;
- man will etwas betonen.

Übersetzung

1. a) Sie reist
2. a) Sie reiste
3. a) Sie ist gereist, Sie reist seit ...
4. a) Sie war gereist.
5. a) Sie wird reisen
6. a) Sie wird gereist sein.
7. a) Sie würde reisen.
8. a) Sie wäre gereist.

Nimmt man anstatt **to travel** z. B. **to sing:**

3. a) Sie hat gesungen. Sie singt seit ...
4. a) Sie hatte gesungen.
6. a) Sie wird gesungen haben.
8. a) Sie hätte gesungen.

Zur Übersetzung der Verlaufsform siehe die Hinweise oben nach III, 8 b.

IV. Translation passage

Read the notes in the solution passage Kap. 7, III first. You don't translate the words in the brackets. They help you to find the correct translation.

1. The tourist relaxed.
2. She will realize the beauty of the island.
3. For (many) years the price of petrol has been rising.
4. He is protesting against the (bad) accomodation
5. Since 1980 he has spent his holidays in Tuscany.
6. I will be phoning my holiday acquaintance.
7. By 1999 I will have visited all the countries of Europe.
8. They would ignore the tourists.
9. They gather the waste.
10. The tourist was kissing his girl-fried.
11. While he was drinking a campari in the bar the telephone rang suddenly.
12. By tomorrow I will have been staying here for three weeks.
13. They had taken this airline.
14. They had been walking in the streets.
15. They would have talked to the native if ...

Die Verlaufsform setzt sich immer mehr durch, weil sie "einfacher" ist. Beachte auch:
Ich bin gegangen. *I have gone (walked, left).*
Sie waren gesprungen. *They had jumped (leapt, leaped).*
Verlaufsorm: I have been going (walking, leaving). They had been jumping (leaping).

V. Make a list of both simple form and progressive form (continuous form), passive

Diese Leideformtabelle erscheint genau so wichtig wie die Tabelle oben, da das Passiv immer Schwierigkeiten bereitet.

1. a) They are welcomed. Sie werden begrüßt (Tatsache).
   b) They are being welcomed. Sie werden (gerade, andauernd, wirklich, extra ...) begrüßt. Vergleiche die Hinweise Kap. 7, III.

2. a) They were welcomed. Sie wurden begrüßt (Tatsache).
   b) They were being welcomed. Sie wurden (gerade ... als, dauernd, wirklich) begrüßt. Vergleiche die Hinweise Kap. 7, III.

3. a) They have been welcomed. Sie sind begrüßt worden, Sie werden begrüßt seit ...
   b) Ab jetzt keine Verlaufsform mehr. Die einfache Form deckt demnach auch den Sinn der Verlaufsform ab.
4. a) They had been welcomed. Sie waren begrüßt worden.
   b) s. o.
5. a) They will be welcomed. Sie werden begrüßt werden. Nicht mit 1a verwechseln!
   b) s. o.
6. a) They will have been welcomed by ... Sie werden bis ... begrüßt (worden) sein.
   b) s. o.
7. a) They would be welcomed. Sie würden begrüßt werden.
   b) s. o.
8. a) They would have been welcomed. Sie wären begrüßt worden. Sie würden begrüßt worden sein.
   b) s. o.

VI. Translation

(Nur die einfache Form verwenden, auch wenn die Verlaufsform möglich wäre!)

1. The environment was threatened.
2. The tax is raised.
3. For 5 years leather handbags have been sold.
4. The rubbish had been gathered.
5. The number of the tourists will be limited.
6. The pollution would be prevented.
7. Everything would have been harmonized.
8. The environment won't be threatened.
9. By 2010 the building won't have been restored.

Kapitel 8

I. Answer the questions on the text in complete sentences

1. The emancipation of women is a typical feature of our century.
2. Women work in almost every trade or profession or vocation, they can vote, they can become members of Parliament.
3. No woman is usually allowed to enter a club.
4. They didn't have enough money as they didn't have enough members.
5. They are still strictly against lady members.
6. In such a club you aren't bothered by daily or emotional problems.
7. You are right as the husband simply wants to forget the problems in such a refuge. You aren't right as the female sex doesn't normally create more problems than the gentlemen when they are among themselves.

II. Answer the additional questions in full sentences as well

1. Both the male, as well as the female sex, i. e. ladies and gentlemen, have the same rights and duties, the same good or bad qualities, the same abilities.
2. A person who is a hardliner, who wants everyone to do what he thinks, who always wants to carry (out) his or her ideas, who always wants to have his or her way.
3. Voters must elect me in a general election provided that I am British.
4. A club like the Garrick is an (exclusive) club where not everybody is admitted. There are regulations which keep improper persons out. There is a rather private or even intimate atmosphere. A tennis club is easier to get into, is rather public and has a special purpose. Think of other sports clubs.
5. A shelter is necessary e. g. in the Alps when there is heavy rain or hail.
6. Not only a husband, everybody! Problems are taxes, rents, extravagant children and women, education problems etc.
7. The clubs are compared with fortresses or bastions and the female sex is like invading or attacking soldiers or troops.

III. Change into the passive

Die Umformung des Aktivsatzes in den Passivsatz ist gar nicht so schwer: Zunächst stellt man Zeit und die Person des Aktivsatzes fest, dann bildet man das Passiv mit der entsprechenden Form von **to be** und dem Mittelwort der Vergangenheit. Im ersten Satz liegt die 3. Person Gegenwart vor. Also heißt das Passiv **is accepted**. Der zweite Schritt ist die Veränderung des Objekts zum Subjekt, aus dem Subjekt wird **by** + Objekt. Letztere Phrase, das **agent,** kann weggelassen werden. Nun die Lösungen mit weiteren Hinweisen:

1. It is accepted by the strictest macho.
2. It will be accepted (by him).
3. That wasn't allowed by the president of the club.
4. The doors have been opened (by some).
5. They haven't been opened (by some).
6. It had been tolerated by us. **Us** ist das Objekt von **we**.
7. A martini is being drunk by the gentlemen. Verlaufsform!
8. The (their) male bastion was being defended by them. **Them** ist das Objekt von **they**.
9. This bill must be rejected. Die Phrase sieht also imme so aus: Hilfszeitwort + **be** + Mittelwort der Vergangenhei (vgl. auch Fragen 10 und 11!
10. It can be rejected (by them).
11. Problems might (could) be kept out by the shelter.
12. Dieser Satz hat zwei Objekte: Das persönliche Objekt **the ladies** und das Sachobjekt **flowers**. Also kann ich auch zwei Passivsätze bilden:
    a) The ladies were given flowers (by the members of the club).
    b) Flowers were given to the ladies by ...
13. a) They have been given the member cards by the president.
    b) The member cards have been given **to** them by ...
14. a) The absent members were sent the cards.
    b) The cards were sent to the absent members.
    In den Sätzen 12 bis 14 wird das Passiv konsequent angewandt.
15. The new female members were looked at by the amused gentlemen. Das Verhältniswort (z. B. **at**) muß auch im Passiv beim Verb bleiben.
16. They weren't laughed at by ... macho (siehe Frage 15!
17. Are the husbands disturbed by their wives?
18. Were their children educated well by them?
19. Has ist been accepted by them?

Bei Frage und Verneinung im Aktiv nur **does** in der Gegenwart, **did** in der 1. Vergangenheit, im Passiv aber immer die entsprechende Form von **to be**! Vergleiche Kap. 7, V und VI.

IV. Complete the list

1. knowledge
2. to emancipate
3. to characterize, character
4. equality, equalisation,
5. prosperity, prosperous
6. to develop
7. strictness
8. to iron, iron
9. entrance, entry
10. thought, thinkeable
11. tolerance
12. defence
13. traditional
14. refusal
15. to envy, envious
16. to argue
17. marriage
18 fanaticism
19. truth (vgl. auch Kap. 2, XI und teilweise Kap. 10, IV.)

V. Definitions

1. It's the release from any power or influence and the equalisation with other groups.
2. A century is a period of a hundred years.
3. A macho thinks men are better than women. He is a person who is proud of being a man.
4. It's a job you usually need special schools or the university for.
5. The P. M. is the leader of the British government, the minister president.
6. An empire is a state which is ruled by an emperor.
7. The majority is a greater number.
8. Jealousy is a (bad) quality. You suffer from realizing (or imagining) that another person is loved more than you.
9. Your wife is your lucky partner!
   Vergleiche Kap. 2, IX; Kap. 3, III; Kap. 4, III.

VI. Ask for the given answers

1. a) Are there many clubs?
2. a) Were they accepted?
3. a) Does he like his club?
4. a) Was he against ladies?
5. a) Did he oppose?
6. a) Has the plan been rejected?
7. a) Must they pay a fee? Do they have to pay a fee? Are they forced to pay a fee? Are they obliged to pay a fee? Are they compelled to pay a fee?
   Beachte die Verneinung von **must!**
8. a) Did the plan have to be turned down?
   Achte auf die Umschreibung mit **do** beziehungsweise **did** bei **to have to = must!**
9. a) Do the ladies have to leave? Must they leave? (vgl. Frage 8 a!)
10. a) Will they come back?

Es ist somit zu beachten, daß bei der Frage im Aktiv immer ein "Umschreibungswort" stehen muß, also

- do, does (present)
- did (past)
- have, has (present perfect)
- had (past perfect)
- will (future)
- will ... have (future perfect)
- would (conditional)
- would ... have (conditional perfect)

Im Passiv steht das entsprechende "Funktionswort". Die Reihenfolge ist die gleiche:

- am, is are
- was, were
- have ... been, has ... been
- had ... been
- will ... be
- will ... have been
- would ... be
- would ... have been

Kapitel 9

I. Answer the questions on the text in complete sentences

1. He founded the (High) Church of England.
   Er gründete die englische Hochkirche oder die anglikanische Kirche. Halte auseinander: **to find, found, found = finden** und **found, founded, founded = gründen!**
2. Generally there is a difference. In our case the prince was charming, but the king of about 50 looked unfriendly and unpleasant.
   Beachte, daß nach **look = aussehen**, das pure Eigenschaftswort steht!
3. He could marry her as his brother Arthur had died ... gestorben war ... Vorzeitigkeit.
4. The kingdom must have a male heir. If not, a civil war might arise.
   ... entsteht eventuell ein Bürger krieg ... **arise, arose, arisen** ...
5. There might have been a crisis in the king's life (see Nr. 4) and Anne Boleyn was young and beautiful.
6. The Queen didn't give birth to a son (see Nr. 4).
7. There were rumours that she was unfaithful.
   ... Gerüchte ... untreu.
8. It was a concession to his former wife.
   ... Zugeständnis ... frühere Ehefrau.
9. His first wife had died and his second (one) had been executed.
   ... war hingerichtet worden, Passiv.
10. He gained a prince but lost his wife.
11. Catherine died later.
12. No, you haven't slipped up, i. e. made a mistake, because Harry was a pet name. They called Henry Great Harry in fact.
    ... Kosename ... Harry is also a pet name for Harold.

II. Answer further questions in full sentences as well

1. I think Henry VIII is such a famous king and it's rather interesting to hear about him. There are films about him. His way of life wasn't usual indeed.
2. They must get their divorce first.
   ... Scheidung ... But mind the numerous problems which arise, e. g. financial problems, who can educate the children, the kids themselves suffer from their parents' divorce ...
   ... leiden unter ...

3. There was a civil war in England between the king and the Parliament, simply between Charles I and Oliver Cromwell. There was a civil war in the U.S.A. between North and South. There is a civil war in Northern Ireland and in Yugoslavia, especially in Bosnia and Herzegovina.
4. It's your new fried. Your former friend has left you or you finished the romance yourself. The successor is undoubtedly much nicer.
   ... Nachfolger ... zweifelsohne ...
5. As he was the head he was able to make the decisions himself
   ... selber entscheiden ...
6. The partner has relations with someone else. ... There is a love affair with another person. You shouldn't do that. See Nr. 2.
7. I can catch a cold in every season if my clothing isn't proper or a room is too cold or when I sit in a draught.
   ... sich erkälten ... Kleidung nicht angemessen ... Zugluft.
8. Two of the king's wives were executed.

III. Translation passage

1. The king had himself portrayed.
   Diese Konstruktion **have** + Objekt + Mittelwort der Vergangenheit sagt aus, daß man etwas durch andere oder von anderen tun läßt.
2. He had the queen executed.
3. He made the princess wait in the room.
   Make + Objekt + Infinitiv ohne **to** sagt aus, daß man jemanden etwas unfreiwillig, ohne daß darum gebeten wurde, tun läßt.
4. He left Anne of Cleves in the room.
   Leave bedeutet **zurücklassen**.
5. My parents let me go to the pictures so that I can see the film **A man for all seasons.**
   Hier will **let** aussagen, daß man jemanden etwas tun läßt, worum er gebeten hat. Vergleiche dazu Nr. 3.
6. Will you have (are you going to have) your hair cut before you go to the cinema?
   Frage im Vergleich zu Nrn. 1 und 2.
7. No, I won't have them cut, I want to have long hair like Anne Boleyn.
   Verneinung zu Nrn. 1 und 2. In Nrn. 6 und 7 ist sinngemäß Zukunft verlangt.

IV. Indirect questions

Es gelten die gleichen Regeln wie beim indirekten Aussagesatz. Zusätzlich ist zu beachten, daß bei den Fragewortfragen das Fragewort natürlich stehenbleiben muß, bei den Entscheidungsfragen **whether** oder **if = ob** vorangestellt wird (vgl. Kap. 5, IV).

1. ... where the portrait painter was who had to paint his portrait".
2. ... when they heard about those rumours ... when they had heard about those rumours.
3. ... who was sent ... that executioner ... who had been sent ... that executioner.
4. ... asked Anne whether she had received flowers the day before ... whether she received ...
5. ... whether we (they) could go hunting ... if they were able to go ...
6. Beliebige Person einsetzen: ... asked her if he might invite her ... whether he was allowed to invite her.
7. ... whether that was the German princess.
8. ... whether I (you, he, she ...) had seen his collection of paintings.
9. ... asked her if she would marry him the following year.
10. ... if they should play the lute.
11. ... if he should sing the song there.

Achte auf die zu verändernden Umstandsangaben! In manchen Fällen mußt du eine angesprochene Person "erfinden"! Die Frageumschreibung entfällt in der indirekten Frage, siehe Nrn. 2 und 4 (vgl. auch Kap. 2, XII; Kap. 6, IV; Kap. 9, V).

V. Tell me what the king ordered

1. ... her to come to the palace.
2. ... them not to show any ...
3. He told her to stay in her chamber.
   Im indirekten Befehlssatz ist **said** durch **told** zu ersetzen. Eine Person erfinden!
4. ... us not to talk about what we had heard.
   Befehle werden einfach zu Infinitiven verändert.
   Vergleiche Kap. 2, XII; Kap. 5, IV; Kap. 6, IV; Kap. 9, V.

VI. Mixed Grammar Passage

1. ... loving
2. going
3. waiting
4. stay ... Ich hielt mich gewöhnlich dort auf.
5. had given birth ... (Bedingungssatz)
6. ... her ... (Objekt + Infinitiv)
7. ... were ... (irrealer Wunschsatz, 1. Vergangenheit)
8. ... extremely ... (Gradangabe)
9. ... writing ... (**-ing**-Form nach **mind**)
10. ... bitter ... (nach **taste** Angabe ohne **-ly).**
11. ... being executed ... (nach **avoid -ing-**Form, hier zudem Passiv)
12. ... to be released ... (Infinitiv Passiv nach **expect)**
13. ... to rescue ... (Infinitiv nach **manage)**
14. ... totally ... (Gradangabe) ... bitterly ... (Umstandsangabe der Art und Weise).

Hinweise:

a) Nach **worth, what about, no use** die ing-Form.
b) zum **if**-Satz siehe Kap. 1, V.
c) Zu Objekt + Infinitiv siehe Kap. 1, III und Kap. 2, IV.
d) Zu Umstandsangaben, Gradangaben, Art-und-Weise-Angaben siehe auch Kap. 3, V und Kap. 6, VII. Die Häufigkeitsangabe, adverb of frequency, z. B. **often, sometimes, always, never** sei hier nur am Rande erwähnt.
e) Zum Infinitv oder zur **-ing**-Form siehe auch Kap. 1, IV und Kap. 4, IV.

Kapitel 10

I. Answer the questions on the text in complete sentences. If you don't you will lose points.

1. It was able to run away as there was a power cut and the cages didn't lock automatically.
2. There was heavy rain which had blotted out the footprints.
3. They telephoned the police as they hadn't found the bear.
4. The police stopped looking for the bear as it got dark.
5. They thought the noise would make the bear confused and aggressive.
6. It was late spring and the leaves hid the bear.
7. A dog and the farmer found the bear eventually.
8. He was the expert then who could cause the bear to come down from the tree.
9. Too much is like a narcosis which causes immediate sleep, too little is dangerous for the men as the bear might attack them.
10. They watched the bear in order to see if the tranquilizer had an effect.
11. A bear has got fur therefore he was a furry escapee.
12. The cage was locked well and he couldn't go for a trip once more.

II. Answer further questions in full sentences as well

1. There isn't any electrical energy any longer as the supply of electricity fails. You can't watch television, you can't listen to the radio, the fridge, the dishwasher don't work. Elevators and lifts, and trams, trolley buses stand still. Even your doorbell doesn't ring.
2. It's a permanent place of entertainment with a lot of facilities. There are merry-go rounds, there are Ferris wheels (the American engineer G. W. G. Ferris built these giant wheels first), you can enter rockets, you can row a boat on a lake, you can ride on ponies and horses (there are many other interesting animals), there is a ghost train, there are huge water slides, there are miniatures of famous sights. Last but not least, there are lots of cafeterias, snack-bars, kiosks. In Seine-et-Marne near Paris there is the biggest amusement park, Euro Disneyland. There you can see Mickey and Goofy and so on.
3. A helicopter is used for taking injured people to hospital, for fighting forest fires, for controlling the traffic on motorways or autobahns.

4. I am confused if the teacher asks me and I haven't the slightest idea or if I don't know what to do or where I am. I get aggressive when somebody does something which I can't stand or tolerate at all.
5. Yes, the Red Indians used blow pipes and many aborigines.
6. I will be surprised if I hear about something which I haven't expected or waited for. I get a present I haven't dreamt of.
7. I must have a blanket to lie on at the swimming baths or to cover myself on a couch.

III. Find synonyms or similar phrases

1. tale
2. proprietor
3. footprints
4. phoned, called
5. went on
6. helpful, suitable
7. in the end, eventually
8. approached
9. in fact
10. everyone
11. it collapsed
12. trip, day out.

Vergleiche Kap. 2, III und Kap. 3, VI.

IV. The corresponding nouns

1. escape, escapee
2. stop
3. difficulty
4. doubt, doubter
5. confusion
6. aggression, aggressor
7. reality
8. sleep
9. strength
10. care, carefulness

In 1, 4 und 6 wurde das persönliche Hauptwort mit aufgeführt (vgl. auch Kap. 2, XI und Kap. 8, IV).

V. Translation passage

1. Because of the leaves you couldn't see the bear.
2. The farmers were needlessly anxious about the cattle especially about their calves because the bear is a vegetarian.
3. But it's not ideal if the bear wants to play with (the) children, if it hugs you the situation will get dangerous.
4. "This is a useful piece of information", the vet said.
5. "Can you give me further information"? the sergeant asked.
6. "You all must obey the advice of the police".
7. This is a good piece of advice, indeed.
8. "This is interesting news." "This is an interesting piece of news", the sergeant said to the farmer.
9. The vet put on his glasses in order to see the dosage better.
10. In the amusement park a lot of animals don't live in pleasant surroundings, (the) police say.

Gerade mit der Übersetzung kann man Grammatik einüben und abfragen. Diese Methode ist gewiß schwieriger als eine Einsetzübung mit "Zufallstreffern". Es geht hier um Besonderheiten der Mehrzahl. Die unregelmäßige Mehrzahl von **leaf** (Nr. 1), **calf** (Nr. 2) und **child** (Nr. 3) ist sicher schon bekannt; siehe auch folgende Tabelle:

Einzahl	**Mehrzahl**	**Einzahl**	**Mehrzahl**
bus	buses	woman	women
glass	glasses	aircraft	aircraft
country	countries	ox	oxen
wolf	wolves	foot	feet

Cattle und **police** gibt es nur als Mehrzahl (Nrn. 2 und 10). Kompliziert wird es bei **information** (Nrn. 4 und 5), **advice** (Nrn. 6 und 7). Hier steht englische Einzahl für deutsche Mehrzahl. **Information** und **advice** entspricht Information**en** und Ratschläg**en**. Will ich eine einzelne Information oder einen einzelnen Rat beschreiben, nehme ich **a piece of, a bit of** oder **an item of** zu Hilfe (Nrn. 4 und 7). Zu dieser Kategorie gehören u. a. auch:

- furniture
- knowledge
- homework
- progress

Beispiel:
The furniture was collected. Die Möbel wurden abgeholt.
Aber: *This piece of furniture is expensive.*
Dieses (eine) Möbel(stück) ist teuer.

Natürlich kann ich auch mehrere Einzelstücke meinen:
- Ich will diese fünf Möbel kaufen.
  I want to buy these five pieces of furniture.
- Ich brauche nur noch zwei Informationen.
  I only need two bits of information.

News steht sowohl für Nachricht als auch für Nachrichten.

Beispiel:
This isn't interesting news.
Dies **sind** keine interessanten Nachrichten.
Dies **ist** keine interessante Nachricht.

Daneben gibt es Begriffe, die englische Mehrzahl haben und im Deutschen nur in der Einzahl gebraucht werden, wie z. B. **glasses,** die Brille, und **surroundings,** die Umgebung. Dazu gehören u. a. auch:
- scissors
- jeans
- trousers
- pyjamas
- shorts
- pliers

Diese Gegenstände haben in der Tat zwei Teile. Meine ich ein Einzelstück, verwende ich die Phrase **a pair of**.

Beispiel:
I want to buy this pair of pyjamas.
Ich möchte diesen Schlafanzug
I need this yellow pair of scissors.
Ich brauche diese gelbe Schere.

Dagegen: Die Jeans ist elegant. *The jeans are elegant.*

VI. Translation Passage

Give the correct relative pronoun.

1. James Green, who is a good vet (erinary), doesn't like interviews.
2. George Hampton, who discovered the bear, has a pretty farm indeed.
3. The vet's daughter, whom I like very much, attends the grammar school.
4. J. G., whose surgery is a bit old-fashioned, is a good vet.
5. Mrs Green, with whom I danced at the grand ball of the fire brigade, might be a good mother-in-law.
6. The vet's jeep, which is in the garage now, cost a lot.
7. Our runaway's cage, whose bars are slightly bent, is in the centre of the amusement park.
8. This amusement park, which belongs to a society, is visited frequently.
9. This cafeteria here, in which I am just sitting, is a good facility in the amusement park.

Das bezügliche Fürwort von Personen ist im Subjekt **who,** im Genitiv **whose,** im Objekt (auch mit Präposition) **whom.**
Sachen lassen sich entsprechend durch **which, whose, which** "vertreten". In unserem Fall ist der Beifügesatz oder Relativsatz ein "nicht notwendiger" Einschub. Jeder Satz ergäbe ja ohne das relative "Zwischenstück" auch Sinn! Man bezeichnet diesen Nebensatz deshalb als nicht-notwendigen Beifügesatz oder **non-restrictive relative cause**. Dieser nicht-notwendige Relativsatz muß durch ein Komma abgetrennt werden.

VII. Translation Passage

Once more the correct relative pronouns. In some cases there are different pronouns possible or you can even leave them out.

1. The men who carried (were carrying) the bear were employees of the owner (proprietor). The men that ...
2. The girl whom I invited on Saturday is the vet's daughter. The girl who I invited ... The girl I invited ... The girl that I invited ...
3. The lady with whom I danced at the fire brigade's grand ball is the vet's wife. The lady who I danced with at ... The lady I danced with ... The lady that I danced with ...
4. The girl who is wearing leggings is her sister. The girl that is ...
5. But the girl in whom I am interested is not her. But she's not the girl who I am interested in ... But she's not the girl I am interested in ... But she's not the girl that I am interested in ...

6. The man whose dog found the bear is a farmer.
7. The job in which I am interested is the profession of the (a) vet. The job which I am interested in is ... The job I am interested in is ... The job that I am interested in is ...
8. That's a job which is very interesting ... a job that ...
9. The book whose contents (the contents of which) fascinated me was a book on animals.
10. Finally I must say that the translation which you are just doing isn't easy at all. ... that the translation that you are just doing ... that the translation you are just doing ...

In diesem Abschnitt ging es um den notwendigen Beifügesatz, **restrictive relative clause.** Er wird ohne Komma eingefügt. Dieser Nebensatz erläutert oder bestimmt das vorhergehende Hauptwort näher. Welche Männer waren Angestellte? Ach ja, die, welche den Bären trugen!

Es gibt mehrere Möglichkeiten, das personale Fürwort **who, whose, whom** zu gebrauchen**:**

- Das **who** kann durch **that** ausgetauscht werden (vgl. Nr. 4).
- Das Objekt **whom** kann durch **who** oder **that** ersetzt oder ganz weggelassen werden (vgl. Nr. 5).

Die Phrase Verhältniswort + Objekt hat ebenfalls Varianten (vgl. Nrn. 3 und 5)

- Verhältniswort + whom
- who ... Verhältniswort nachgestell
- ganz weglassen ...Verhältniswort nachgestellt
- **that** ... Verhältniswort nachgestellt

Diese Regeln gelten auch für das sächliche Fürwort **which, whose, which.** Auch hier ist das Objekt **which** und die Phrase Verhältniswort + **which**, variabel (vgl. Nr. 7 und 10).
That ist immer möglich.

VIII. A special exercise on helping verbs or auxiliaries

Find all the synonyms or synonymous phrases with them. Once more a translation passage:

1. You must lock (up) the cage ... You have to lock ... You are forced to lock ... You are obliged to lock ... You are compelled to lock ...
2. He needn't feed the ponies today ... He doesn't have to feed ... He isn't forced to ... He isn't compelled to ...

3. He mustn't ride the ponies ... He may not ride ... He isn't allowed to ride ... He isn't permitted to ride ... He can't ride ...
4. She can visit the park ... She is able to visit the ... She may visit ... She is allowed to ... She is permitted to ...
5. We may wait in the cafeteria ... We are allowed to wait in the ... We are permitted to wait ... We can wait ...
6. You should drink only mineral water ... You ought to drink ...
7. They ought to fetch the horses now.
8. I couldn't ride ... I wouldn't be able to ..
9. You are to brush the pony. You are told to brush ... You are supposed to ... You are expected to ... you are said to ...
10. Yesterday the vet was to come ... the vet was expected to come ... the vet was supposed to come ...
11. The vet is said to have a pretty daughter.
12. She is said to be getting married tomorrow ... She is expected to ... She is supposed to ...
13. He is expected to arrive at 9 o'clock.
14. Shall I leave? Am I to leave? Am I expected to leave? Am I supposed to leave? Am I told to leave?
15. I want to see the park. I am willing to see the park. I intend to ... I wish to ...

Diese Übung hat's in sich, daher hier noch einige Hinweise zu den einzelnen Aufgaben (1 bis 15):

1. Natürlich besitzen die einzelnen Phrasen eine unterschiedliche Intensität. Am schwächsten ist **to have to,** am stärksten **to be forced to**.
2. **Must not** wäre falsch gewesen.
3. Hier steht must not.
4. Can und Ersatzwort
   - als Fähigkeit
   - als Erlaubnis
5. **can** auch als Erlaubnis
6. Gegenwart!
7. Gegenwart!
8. vgl. Kap. 10, XI, Hinweise
9. **to be to** als Ersatzform, **shall** nur bei Frage in der 1. Person;
   - es wird ihr gesagt (befohlen) ...
   - man erwartet es ...
   - man vermutet es ...
   - man sagt es ...

10. 1. Vergangenheit von **to be to** (vgl. auch Nrn. 6 und 9)
11. man sagt es
12. man sagt es ...; man erwartet es ...; man vermutet es ...
13. man erwartet es
14. nur in der 1. Person Frage **shall** möglich. Es folgen die anderen (siehe oben) Ersatzformen.
15. **will** vermeiden, dafür Ersatzformen.

IX. Put Nr. 1, 4, 5, 6, 9, 15 into the negative. See the solutions first:

1. You needn't lock ... You don't have to ... You aren't forced to ... You aren't obliged to ... You aren't compelled to lock.
4. She can't visit ... She isn't able to visit ... She mustn't visit ... She may not visit ... She isn't allowed to visit ... She isn't permitted to visit ...
5. We may not wait ... We mustn't wait ... We aren't allowed to wait ... We aren't permittet to wait ... We can't wait ...
6. You shouldn't drink ... You oughtn't to drink ...
9. You aren't to brush the pony. You aren't told to ... You aren't supposed to ... You aren't expected to ... You aren't said to ...
15. I don't want to see the park ... I am not willing to see ... I don't intend to ... I don't wish to see ...

X. Make a list of Kap. 10, VIII, Nr. 4

1. **Present** (Gegenwart):
   She can visit ... She is able to ... She may visit ... She is allowed to visit ... She is permitted to visit ..
2. **Past** (1. Vergangenheit):
   She was able to visit ... She was allowed to visit ... She was permitted to visit ...
3. **Present Perfect** (2. Vergangenheit):
   She has been able to visit ... She has been allowed to ... She has been permitted to ...
4. **Past Perfect** (3. Vergangenheit):
   She had been able to visit ... She had been allowed to ... She had been permitted to ...
5. **Future** (1. Zukunft):
   She will be able to ... She will be allowed to ... She will be permittet do ...
6. **Future Perfect** (2. Zukunft) gibt keinen Sinn.

XI. Shift into past beginning with "Yesterday ..."

1. Yesterday I had to lock ... I was forced to lock ... I was compelled to lock ... I was obliged to lock ...
2. Yesterday you didn't have to feed ... You weren't forced to ... you weren't compelled to ... You weren't obliged to ...
3. Yesterday he was able to wait there ... he was allowed to wait ... He was permitted to wait...
4. Yesterday she couldn't wait ... she wasn't able to wait ... she wasn't allowed to wait ... she wasn't permitted to wait ..
5. Yesterday we were allowed to leave the ... we were permitted ...
6. Yesterday you weren't allowed to enter ... you weren't permitted to ... You couldn't enter ...

Hinweise:

Du hast festgestellt, daß die Hilfszeitworte **must, may, needn't** und **mustn't** nicht in die tatsächliche Vergangenheit verschoben werden können.

Nur in der Verneinung und Frage kann **could** in der Regel auch **konnte** bedeuten; sonst ist **could** mit **könnte** zu übersetzen (vgl. Kap. 10, VIII, 8).

In der indirekten Rede (siehe Kap. 2, XII; Kap. 5, IV; Kap. 6, IV) können **Vergangenheitsformen** von **may, shall** und **can** gebildet werden: might, should, could.

Anhang

Tabelle 1: Bezeichnung der Zeiten

Deutsch	**Fremdwort**	**Englisch**
Gegenwart	Präsens	Present
1. Vergangenheit	Präteritum /Imperfekt	Past
2. Vergangenheit	Perfekt	Present Perfect
3. Vergangenheit	Plusquamperfekt	Past Perfect
1. Zukunft	Futur	Future
2. Zukunft	Futur Perfekt	Future Perfect
1. Bedingungsform	Konditional	Conditional
2. Bedingungsform	Konditional Perfekt	Conditional Perfect

Tabelle 2: Grammatikglossar

Deutsch	**Fremdwort**	**Englisch**	**Beispiel**
Hauptwort	Nomen	Noun	girl
Eigenschaftswort	Adjektiv	Adjective	beautiful
Zeitwort/Tunwort	Verb	Verb	to sing
Geschlechtswort	Artikel	Article	the, a
Besitzanzeigendes Fürwort	Possessivpronomen	Possessive Pronoun	my, his, their
Hinweisendes Fürwort	Demonstrativpronomen	Demonstrative Pronoun	this, that, these, those
Bezügliches Fürwort	Relativpronomen	Relative Pronoun	who, whose, that, which
Rückbezügliches Fürwort	Reflexivpronomen	Reflexive Pronoun	allgemein: oneself; myself, themselves
Betonendes Fürwort		Emphasizing Pronoun	(gleiche Form wie rückbez. Fürwort)
Wechselbezügliches Fürwort		Reciprocal Pronoun	each other, one another
Verhältniswort	Präposition	Preposition	on, in, with
Bindewort	Konjunktion	Conjunction	as, before, after
Steigerung	Komparativ, Superlativ	Comparative, Superlative	greater, more famous, biggest, most elegant
Zeit	Tempus	Tense	Present, Past

Deutsch	**Fremdwort**	**Englisch**	**Beispiel**
Tatform	Aktiv	Active (Voice)	I sing
Leideform	Passiv	Passive (Voice)	The song **is sung**
(Umstands-) Angabe	Adverb, Adverbiale	Adverb	(einzelne Beispiele folgen:)
Zeitangabe	Temporaladverbiale	Adverb of Time	yesterday, in May
Ortsangabe	Lokaladverbiale	Adverb of Place	here, in London
Art und Weise	Modaladverbiale	Adverb of Manner	slowly, quickly, fast
Gradangabe		Adverb of Degree	very, extremely
Intensitätsangabe		Adverb of Degree	totally, fully
Häufigkeitsangabe	z. T. Temporal-adverbiale	Adverb of Frequency	sometimes, always
Satzergänzung	Objekt	Object	I like **English**
Satzgegenstand	Subjekt	Subject	**Peter** hates English
Satzaussage	Prädikat	Verb, Predicate	She **reads** a book
Hilfszeitwort	Modalverb	Auxiliary, Helping Verb	can, may, must

Tabelle 3 a: to cook – kochen (Aktiv): Beispiel für ein "normales" Zeitwort im Aktiv

	Present	Past	Present Perf.	Past Perfect	Future	Future Perf.	Conditional	Condit. Perf.
Aussage-satz	I cook *Ich koche*	I cooked *Ich kochte*	I have cooked *Ich habe gekocht; ich koche seit ...*	I had cooked *Ich hatte gekocht*	I will cook *Ich werde kochen*	I will have cooked (by ...) *Ich werde gekocht haben (bis ...)*	I would cook *Ich würde kochen*	I would have cooked *Ich würde ge-kocht haben; ich hätte ...*
	He cooks *Er kocht*	He cooked *Er kochte*	He has cooked *Er hat gekocht; er kocht seit ...*	He had cooked *Er hatte gekocht*	He will cook *Er wird kochen*	He will have cooked (by ...) *Er wird ge-kocht haben (bis ...)*	He would cook *Er würde kochen*	He would have cooked *Er würde ge-kocht haben; er hätte ...*
Verneinung	I don't cook *Ich koche nicht*	I didn't cook *Ich kochte nicht*	I haven't cooked *Ich habe nicht gekocht; ich koche nicht seit ...*	I hadn't cooked *Ich hatte nicht ge-kocht*	I won't cook *Ich werde nicht kochen*	I won't have cooked *Ich werde nicht gekocht haben*	I wouldn't cook *Ich würde nicht kochen*	I wouldn't have cooked *Ich würde nicht gekocht haben; ich hätte nicht ...*
	He doesn't cook *Er kocht nicht*	He didn't cook *Er kochte nicht*	He hasn't cooked *Er hat nicht gekocht; er kocht nicht seit ...*	He hadn't cooked *Er hatte nicht ge-kocht*	He won't cook *Er wird nicht kochen*	He won't have cooked *Er wird nicht gekocht haben*	He wouldn't cook *Er würde nicht kochen*	He wouldn't have cooked *Er würde nicht gekocht haben; er hätte nicht ...*
Frage	Do you cook? *Kochst du?*	Did you cook? *Kochtest du?*	Have you cooked ? *Hast du gekocht? Kochst du seit ...?*	Had you cooked? *Hattest du gekocht?*	Will you cook? *Wirst du kochen?*	Will you have cooked? *Wirst du ge-kocht haben?*	Would you cook? *Würdest du kochen?*	Would you have cooked? *Würdest du gekocht haben? Hättest du ...?*
	Does he cook? *Kocht er?*	Did he cook? *Kochte er?*	Has he cooked? *Hat er ge-kocht? Kocht er seit ...?*	Had he cooked? *Hatte er gekocht?*	Will he cook? *Wird er kochen?*	Will he have cooked? *Wird er ge-kocht haben?*	Would he cook? *Würde er kochen?*	Would he have cooked? *Würde er ge-kocht haben? Hätte er ...?*

Tabelle 3 b: to cook – kochen: Verlaufsform im Aktiv

Zur Übersetzung siehe Verlaufsform im Aktiv (Tabelle 5 b, 6 und Kap. 7, C. III)

	Present	Past	Present Perfect	Past Perfect	Future	Future Perfect	Conditional	Conditional Perfect
Aussagesatz	I am cooking	I was cooking	I have been cooking	I had been cooking	I will be cooking	I will have been cooking	I would be cooking	I would have been cooking
	You are cooking	You were cooking	You have been cooking	You had been cooking	You will be cooking	You will have been cooking	You would be cooking	You would have been cooking
	He is cooking	He was cooking	He has been cooking	He had been cooking	He will be cooking	He will have been cooking	He would be cooking	He would have been cooking
Verneinung	I'm not cooking	I wasn't cooking	I haven't been cooking	I hadn't been cooking	I won't be cooking	I won't have been cooking	I wouldn't be cooking	I wouldn't have been cooking
	You aren't cooking	You weren't cooking	You haven't been cooking	You hadn't been cooking	You won't be cooking	You won't have been cooking	You wouldn't be cooking	You wouldn't have been cooking
	He isn't cooking	He wasn't cooking	He hasn't been cooking	He hadn't been cooking	He won't be cooking	He won't have been cooking by	He wouldn't be cooking	He wouldn't have been cooking
Frage	Are you cooking?	Were you cooking?	Have you been cooking?	Had you been cooking?	Will you be cooking?	Will you have been cooking?	Would you be cooking?	Would you have been cooking?
	Is he cooking?	Was he cooking?	Has he been cooking?	Had he been cooking?	Will he be cooking?	Will he have been cooking?	Would he be cooking?	Would he have been cooking?

Tabelle 4: to be against – sich dagegen wenden: Beispiel für ein Zeitwort mit "to be"

3. Person Singular

	Present	**Past**	**Present Perfect**	**Past Perfect**	**Future**	**Future Perfect**	**Conditional**	**Conditional Perfect**
Aussage-satz	He is against *Er wendet sich da-gegen*	He was against *Er wandte sich da-gegen*	He has been against *Er hat sich dagegen gewandt; er wendet sich dagegen seit ...*	He had been against *Er hatte sich dagegen ge-wandt*	He will be against *Er wird sich da-gegen wenden*	He will have been against *Er wird sich (bis ...) dagegen gewandt haben*	He would be against *Er würde sich dagegen wenden*	He would have been against *Er würde sich dagegen ge-wandt haben; er hätte sich dagegen gewandt*
Verneinung	He isn't against *Er wendet sich nicht dagegen*	He wasn't against *Er wandte sich nicht dagegen*	He hasn't been against *Er hat sich nicht dagegen gewandt; er wendet sich nicht dagegen seit ...*	He hadn't been against *Er hatte sich nicht dage-gen gewandt*	He won't be against *Er wird sich nicht dagegen wenden*	He won't have been against *Er wird sich (bis ...) nicht dagegen ge-wandt haben*	He wouldn't be against *Er würde sich nicht dagegen wenden*	He wouldn't have been against *Er würde sich nicht dagegen gewandt haben; er hätte sich nicht ...*
Frage	Is he against? *Wendet er sich da-gegen?*	Was he against? *Wandte er sich dagegen?*	Has he been against? *Hat er sich dagegen gewandt? Wendet er sich dagegen seit ...?*	Had he been against? *Hatte er sich dagegen ge-wandt?*	Will he be against? *Wird er sich da-gegen wenden?*	Will he have been against? *Wird er sich (bis ...) dage-gen gewandt haben?*	Would he be against? *Würde er sich dagegen wenden?*	Would he have been against? *Würde er sich dagegen ge-wandt haben? Hätte er sich dagegen gewandt?*

1. Person Plural

	Present	Past	Present Perfect	Past Perfect	Future	Future Perfect	Conditional	Conditional Perfect
Aussage-satz	They are against *Sie wenden sich dagegen*	They were against *Sie wandten sich dagegen*	They have been against *Sie haben sich dagegen gewandt; sie wenden sich dagegen seit ...*	They had been against *Sie hatten sich dagegen gewandt*	They will be against *Sie werden sich dagegen wenden*	They will have been against *Sie werden sich (bis ...) dagegen gewandt haben*	They would be against *Sie würden sich dagegen wenden*	They would have been against *Sie würden sich dagegen gewandt haben; sie hätten sich ...*
Verneinung	They aren't against *Sie wenden sich nicht dagegen*	They weren't against *Sie wandten sich nicht dagegen*	They haven't been against *Sie haben sich nicht dagegen gewandt; sie wenden sich nicht dagegen seit ...*	They hadn't been against *Sie hatten sich nicht dagegen gewandt*	They won't be against *Sie werden sich nicht dagegen wenden*	They won't have been against *Sie werden sich (bis ...) nicht dagegen gewandt haben*	They wouldn't be against *Sie würden sich nicht dagegen wenden*	They wouldn't have been against *Sie würden sich nicht dagegen gewandt haben; sie hätten sich nicht ...*
Frage	Are they against? *Wenden sie sich dagegen?*	Were they against? *Wandten sie sich dagegen?*	Have they been against? *Haben sie sich dagegen gewandt?* *Wenden sie sich dagegen seit ...?*	Had they been against? *Hatten sie sich dagegen gewandt?*	Will they be against? *Werden sie sich dagegen wenden?*	Will they have been against? *Werden sie sich (bis ...) dagegen gewandt haben?*	Would they be against? *Würden sie sich dagegen wenden?*	Would they have been against? *Würden sie sich dagegen gewandt haben; hätten sie sich ...*

Tabelle 5 a: to examine – untersuchen: Beispiel für die einfache Form des Passivs

3. Person Singular

	Present	**Past**	**Present Perfect**	**Past Perfect**	**Future**	**Future Perfect**	**Conditional**	**Conditional Perfect**
Aussagesatz	He is examined *Er wird untersucht*	He was examined *Er wurde untersucht*	He has been examined *Er ist untersucht worden; er wird untersucht seit ...*	He had been examined *Er war untersucht worden*	He will be examined *Er wird untersucht werden*	He will have been examined *Er wird (bis ...) untersucht (worden) sein*	He would be examined *Er würde untersucht werden*	He would have been examined *Er würde untersucht worden sein; er wäre untersucht worden*
Verneinung	He isn't examined *Er wird nicht untersucht*	He wasn't examined *Er wurde nicht untersucht*	He hasn't been examined *Er ist nicht untersucht worden; er wird nicht untersucht seit ...*	He hadn't been examined *Er war nicht untersucht worden*	He won't be examined *Er wird nicht untersucht werden*	He won't have been examined *Er wird (bis ...) nicht untersucht (worden) sein*	He wouldn't be examined *Er würde nicht untersucht werden*	He wouldn't have been examined *Er würde nicht untersucht worden sein; er wäre nicht untersucht worden*
Frage	Is he examined? *Wird er untersucht?*	Was he examined? *Wurde er untersucht?*	Has he been examined? *Ist er untersucht worden? Wird er untersucht seit ...?*	Had he been examined? *War er untersucht worden?*	Will he be examined? *Wird er untersucht werden?*	Will he have been examined? *Wird er (bis ...) untersucht (worden) sein?*	Would he be examined? *Würde er untersucht werden?*	Would he have been examined? *Würde er untersucht worden sein? Wäre er untersucht worden?*

1. Person Plural

	Present	Past	Present Perfect	Past Perfect	Future	Future Perfect	Conditional	Conditional Perfect
Aussage-satz	They are examined *Sie werden untersucht*	They were examined *Sie wurden untersucht*	They have been examined *Sie sind unter-sucht worden; sie werden untersucht seit ...*	They had been examined *Sie waren untersucht worden*	They will be examined *Sie werden untersucht werden*	They will have been examined *Sie werden (bis ...) untersucht (worden) sein*	They would be examined *Sie würden untersucht werden*	They would have been examined *Sie würden untersucht worden sein; sie wären untersucht worden*
Verneinung	They aren't examined *Sie werden nicht unter-sucht*	They weren't examined *Sie wurden nicht unter-sucht*	They haven't been examined *Sie sind nicht untersucht worden; sie werden nicht untersucht seit ...*	They hadn't been examined *Sie waren nicht untersucht worden*	They won't be examined *Sie werden nicht untersucht werden*	They won't have been examined *Sie werden (bis ...) nicht untersucht (worden) sein*	They wouldn't be examined *Sie würden nicht unter-sucht werden*	They wouldn't have been examined *Sie würden nicht untersucht worden sein; sie wären nicht untersucht worden*
Frage	Are they examined? *Werden sie untersucht?*	Were they examined? *Wurden sie untersucht?*	Have they been examined ...? *Sind sie unter-sucht worden? Werden sie untersucht seit ...?*	Had they been examined? *Waren sie untersucht worden?*	Will they be examined? *Werden sie untersucht werden?*	Will they have been examined? *Werden sie (bis ...) untersucht (worden) sein*	Would they be examined? *Würden sie untersucht werden?*	Would they have been examined? *Würden sie untersucht worden sein? Wären sie untersucht worden?*

Tabelle 5 b: to examine – untersuchen: Beispiel für die Verlaufsform des Passivs

	Präsens (Present)	**Präteritum (Past)**
Aussagesatz	She is being examined. *Sie wird (gerade, wirklich, intensiv, ununterbrochen usw.) untersucht.* They are being examined. *Sie werden (gerade, wirklich, intensiv, ununterbrochen usw.) untersucht.*	She was being examined. *Sie wurde (gerade, wirklich, intensiv, ununterbrochen usw.) untersucht.* They were being examined. *Sie wurden (gerade, wirklich, intensiv, ununterbrochen usw.) untersucht.*
Verneinung	She isn't being examined. *Sie wird (gerade) nicht (intensiv, ununterbrochen usw.) untersucht.* They aren't being examined. *Sie werden (gerade) nicht (intensiv, ununterbrochen usw.) untersucht.*	She wasn't being examined. *Sie wurde (gerade) nicht (intensiv, ununterbrochen usw.) untersucht.* They weren't being examined. *Sie wurden (gerade) nicht (intensiv, ununterbrochen usw.) untersucht.*
Frage	Is she being examined? *Wird sie (gerade, wirklich, intensiv, ununterbrochen usw.) untersucht?* Are they being examined? *Werden sie (gerade, wirklich, intensiv, ununterbrochen usw.) untersucht?*	Was she being examined? *Wurde sie (gerade, wirklich, intensiv, ununterbrochen usw.) untersucht?* Were they being examined? *Wurden sie (gerade, wirklich, intensiv, ununterbrochen usw.) untersucht?*

Zu den anderen Zeitstufen gibt es keine Verlaufsform (zur Übersetzung der Verlaufsform vgl. auch Kap. 7, B. III).

Tabelle 6: to lay the table – den Tisch decken: Übersicht über Einfache Form + Verlaufsform

1. Aussagesatz

	Present	**Past**	**Present Perfect**	**Past Perfect**	**Future**	**Future Perfect**	**Conditional**	**Conditional Perfect**
a) Einfache Form im Aktiv	He lays the table *Er deckt den Tisch*	He laid the table *Er deckte den Tisch*	He has laid the table *Er hat den Tisch gedeckt*	He had laid the table *Er hatte den Tisch gedeckt*	He will lay the table *Er wird den Tisch decken*	He will have laid the table *Er wird den Tisch (bis ...) gedeckt haben*	He would lay the table *Er würde den Tisch decken*	He would have laid the table *Er hätte den Tisch gedeckt*
b) Verlaufsform im Aktiv	He is laying the table	He was laying the table	He has been laying the table	He had been laying the table	He will be laying the table	He will have been laying the table	He would be laying the table	He would have been laying the table
	Die Verlaufsform kann wie die einfache Form übersetzt werden, nur mit den geschriebenen oder gedachten Einfügungen wie gerade, wirklich, ununterbrochen, extra usw. (vgl. dazu auch Kap. 7, C. III und Tabelle 5 b).							
c) Einfache Form im Passiv	The table is laid *Der Tisch wird gedeckt*	The table was laid *Der Tisch wurde gedeckt*	The table has been laid *Der Tisch ist gedeckt worden*	The table had been laid *Der Tisch war gedeckt worden*	The table will be laid *Der Tisch wird gedeckt werden*	The table will have been laid *Der Tisch wird gedeckt (worden) sein*	The table would be laid *Der Tisch würde gedeckt werden*	The table would have been laid *Der Tisch wäre gedeckt worden*
b) Verlaufsform im Passiv	The table is being laid *(s. o. Verlaufsform im Aktiv)*	The table was being laid *(s. o. Verlaufsform im Aktiv)*						

2. Verneinung

	Present	**Past**	**Present Perfect**	**Past Perfect**	**Future**	**Future Perfect**	**Conditional**	**Conditional Perfect**
a) Einfache Form im Aktiv	He doesn't lay the table *Er deckt den Tisch nicht*	He didn't lay the table *Er deckte den Tisch nicht*	He hasn't laid the table *Er hat den Tisch nicht gedeckt*	He hadn't laid the table *Er hatte den Tisch nicht gedeckt*	He won't lay the table *Er wird den Tisch nicht decken*	He won't have laid the table *Er wird den Tisch (bis ...) nicht gedeckt haben*	He wouldn't lay the table *Er würde den Tisch nicht decken*	He wouldn't have laid the table *Er hätte den Tisch nicht gedeckt*
b) Verlaufs-form im Aktiv	He isn't laying the table	He wasn't laying the table	He hasn't been laying the table	He hadn't been laying the table	He won't be laying the table	He won't have been laying the table	He wouldn't be laying the table	He wouldn't have been laying the table
	Die Verlaufsform kann wie die einfache Form übersetzt werden, nur mit den geschriebenen oder gedachten Einfügungen wie gerade, wirklich, ununterbrochen, extra usw. (vgl. dazu auch Kap. 7, C. III und Tabelle 5 b).							
c) Einfache Form im Passiv	The table isn't laid *Der Tisch wird nicht gedeckt*	The table wasn't laid *Der Tisch wurde nicht gedeckt*	The table hasn't been laid *Der Tisch ist nicht gedeckt worden*	The table hadn't been laid *Der Tisch war nicht gedeckt worden*	The table won't be laid *Der Tisch wird nicht gedeckt werden*	The table won't have been laid *Der Tisch wird (bis ...) nicht gedeckt (worden) sein*	The table wouldn't be laid *Der Tisch würde nicht gedeckt werden*	The table wouldn't have been laid *Der Tisch wäre nicht gedeckt worden*
b) Verlaufs-form im Passiv	The table isn't being laid *(s. o. Verlaufs-form im Aktiv*	The table wasn't being laid *(s. o. Verlaufs-form im Aktiv*						

3. Frage

	Present	Past	Present Perfect	Past Perfect	Future	Future Perfect	Conditional	Conditional Perfect
a) Einfache Form im Aktiv	Does he lay the table? *Deckt er den Tisch?*	Did he lay the table? *Deckte er den Tisch?*	Has he laid the table? *Hat er den Tisch gedeckt?*	Had he laid the table? *Hatte er den Tisch gedeckt?*	Will he lay the table? *Wird er den Tisch decken?*	Will he have laid the table? *Wird er den Tisch (bis ...) gedeckt haben?*	Would he lay the table? *Würde er den Tisch decken?*	Would he have laid the table? *Hätte er den Tisch gedeckt?*
b) Verlaufsform im Aktiv	Is he laying the table?	Was he laying the table?	Has he been laying the table?	Had he been laying the table?	Will he be laying the table?	Will he have been laying the table?	Would he be laying the table?	Would he have been laying the table?
	Die Verlaufsform kann wie die einfache Form übersetzt werden, nur mit den geschriebenen oder gedachten Einfügungen wie gerade, wirklich, ununterbrochen, extra usw. (vgl. dazu auch Kap. 7, C. III und Tabelle 5 b).							
c) Einfache Form im Passiv	Is the table laid? *Wird der Tisch gedeckt?*	Was the table laid? *Wurde der Tisch gedeckt?*	Has the table been laid? *Ist der Tisch gedeckt worden?*	Had the table been laid? *War der Tisch gedeckt worden?*	Will the table be laid? *Wird der Tisch gedeckt werden?*	Will the table have been laid? *Wird der Tisch (bis ...) gedeckt (worden) sein?*	Would the table be laid? *Würde der Tisch gedeckt werden?*	Would the table have been laid? *Wäre der Tisch gedeckt worden?*
b) Verlaufsform im Passiv	Is the table being laid? *(s. o. Verlaufsform im Aktiv*	Was the table being laid? *(s. o. Verlaufsform im Aktiv*						

Stichwortverzeichnis

Bitte hier abtrennen

Der Absender ist:

- ☐ Lehrer
- ☐ Fachbetreuer
- ☐ Oberstufenbetreuer
- ☐ Schulleiter
- ☐ Beratungslehrer
- ☐ Regierungsfachberater
- ☐ Sekretariat
- ☐ Schüler
- ☐ Buchhändler

an:

- ☐ Gymnasium/ Gesamtschule
- ☐ Berufl. Gymnasium/ BOS
- ☐ Fachoberschule
- ☐ Realschule
- ☐ Wirtschaftsschule
- ☐ Hauptschule
- ☐ Teilhauptschule
- ☐ Grundschule
- ☐ Berufskolleg

Zutreffendes bitte ankreuzen!

- ☐ Berufsaufbauschule
- ☐ Berufsfachschule
- ☐ Berufsschule
- ☐ Fachschule
- ☐ Sonderschule
- ☐ Fachhochschule
- ☐ Universität
- ☐ Forschungsinstitut
- ☐ Volkshochschule
- ☐ Sonstige Schulen

Unterrichtsfächer:

Stark Verlag
Postfach 1852
85318 Freising

4-VA

Bitte ausfüllen und im frankierten Umschlag an uns einsenden. Für Fensterkuverts geeignet.

Absender **(bitte in Druckbuchstaben)**

Name/Vorname

Straße/Nr.

PLZ/Ort

Bundesland

Schule/Schulstempel **(bitte unbedingt angeben)**

(Bitte blättern Sie um)

Erörterung 9./10. Klasse
Anleitung zur Erstellung von Gliederungen für die Erörterung anhand von Aufsatzbeispielen. Hinweise auf formale Gestaltung, Sprachrichtigkeit und häufige Fehlerquellen. Mit vielen Übungen und Lösungen sowie Mustergliederungen.
■ **Best.-Nr. 80401** **DM 12,90**

Englisch

Wortschatzübung Englisch Mittelstufe
Nach Wortfamilien geordnet, die wichtigsten Wörter mit Angabe der synonyms und opposites. Dazu ein Leitfaden „Wie erlerne, wiederhole und erschließe ich einen Wortschatz" und Hinweise auf häufige Fehlerquellen.
■ **Best.-Nr. 91455** **DM 14,90**

Translation Practice 1
Intensives Training von Übersetzungen aus dem Englischen. Darstellung der wichtigsten Grammatikbereiche. Dazu Übungssätze mit Übersetzungsmöglichkeiten und 245 Aufgaben mit Lösungen.
■ **Best.-Nr. 80451** **DM 14,90**

Translation Practice 2
Hier wird das Übersetzen ganzer Texte aus dem Englischen mit Hilfestellungen geübt. Dazu Wörterbucharbeit, Übungen zu britischem/amerikanischem Englisch und Lösungen.
■ **Best.-Nr. 80452** **DM 14,90**

Englische Rechtschreibung
Wort- und Satzbeispiele, Darstellung der Regeln und Gesetzmäßigkeiten wie Groß-und Kleinschreibung, Vor- und Nachsilben, unregelmäßige Verbformen, Apostroph-s. 265 Aufgaben mit Lösungen.
■ **Best.-Nr. 80453** **DM 14,90**

Comprehension 1
Übungstexte ab der 8. Klasse. Dazu Fragen, Lösungen, Grammatikübungen, Hinweise auf häufige Fehlerquellen, Wortschatzaufgaben.
■ **Best.-Nr. 91453** **DM 12,90**

Comprehension 2
Übungstexte ab der 9. Klasse. Dazu Fragen, Lösungen, Grammatikübungen, Hinweise auf häufige Fehlerquellen, Übersichtstabellen.
■ **Best.-Nr. 91452** **DM 12,90**

Latein

Latein Wiederholung
Kurzgrammatik zur effektiven Wiederholung der lateinischen Sprache. Übersichtliche Darstellung der Formenlehre, Syntax, Satzanalyse, Stilmittel. Dazu Aufgaben mit erklärenden Lösungen.
■ **Best.-Nr. 94601** **DM 14,90**

Lateinische Literaturgeschichte
Situationsbeschreibungen und chronologischer Überblick, Leben und Werk wichtiger Autoren vor dem Hintergrund der politischen, sozialen und kulturellen Geschichte Roms. Dazu eine kurze Einführung in die lateinische Metrik.
■ **Best.-Nr. 94602** **DM 16,90**

Biologie

Viel Platz für kleine Tiere
Dieser Band beschreibt mit vielen Abbildungen, praktischen Beispielen und hilfreichen Hinweisen, wie jeder den kleinen Wildtieren unserer Heimat viel Platz zum Leben und Überleben bieten kann. Ein ideales Lehr- und Projektbuch zur Gestaltung eines lebendigen Biologieunterrichts.
■ **Best.-Nr. 10479** **DM 12,90**

Bestimmungsschlüssel zur Fließgewässerunteruschung
Dieser Bestimmungschlüssel mit Protokollbögen ermöglicht den Einstieg in die Bestimmung der häufigen Bioindikatoren. Eine einfach nachzuvollziehende Methode und pädagogisch wertvolle Arbeitshilfe für den Biologieunterricht.
■ **Best.-Nr. 84703** **DM 8,90**

Bitte Bestellungen direkt an den Stark Verlag
Postfach 1852 · 85318 Freising · Tel. (08161) 1790 · FAX (08161) 17951
Preisänderungen behalten wir uns vor.

STARK